"I have come not to teach but to awaken."

DISCOURSES

by

Meher Baba

Vol. II

MASTERY
IN SERVITUDE

Discourses by Meher Baba

6th Edition

Library of Congress Catalog Card Number: 67–21136

First printing; October 1967
Second printing; September 1968
Third printing; September 1970
Fourth printing; October 1971
Fifth printing; December 1973

Printed in U.S.A. by Kingsport Press

The present three-volume edition of Meher Baba's original five-volume work is being published by Sufism Reoriented by express permission of Meher Baba, and under licence of his secretary, Adi K. Irani. Meher Baba wished this earlier edition revised in order to make certain corrections supplied by him. The editorial revisions and arrangement of chapters was also approved.

The Editors

Introduction

Merwan Sheriar Irani was born in Poona, India, on February 25, 1894. His parents were of Persian extraction. His father, Sheriar Irani, was a persistent seeker of God.

Merwan was a lively and happy boy who excelled in both studies and sports. In 1913 while in his first year at Poona's Deccan College he met the aged Muslim saint Hazrat Babajan, one of the five Perfect Masters of the time. Being attracted to her, he visited her from time to time and one day she kissed him on the forehead, revealing to him his state of God-realization.

At first Merwan was dazed but gradually the focus of his consciousness returned sufficiently to his surroundings to lead him to the *Qutub-i-Irshad*, Sai Baba, who in turn sent him to another Perfect Master, the Hindu, Upasni Maharaj of Sakori. For seven years Upasni Maharaj integrated Merwan's God-consciousness with consciousness of the mundane world, preparing him for his role as the Avatar of the Age. This avataric mission started in 1921 with the gathering together of his first disciples, who gave him the name "Meher Baba" or "Compassionate Father."

After years of intensive work with these disciples, and travel in India and Persia (Iran), Meher Baba established quarters at an old military camp near

Ahmednagar. This became known as Meherabad. Here he instituted a number of pilot plant projects such as a free hospital and dispensary, shelters for the poor and a free school where spiritual training was stressed. In the school no caste lines were observed, as the high and the low mingled in common fellowship forged by love of the Master. To all Baba offered regular instruction in moral discipline, love for God, spiritual understanding and selfless service.

All these activities moved at high speed despite Baba's silence, which he announced with little advance warning and commenced on July 10, 1925. At first he communicated by pointing to letters on an alphabet board, but in 1954 he gave up even this device. He now converses through his own unique shorthand system of representative gestures. Both *Discourses* and *God Speaks*, however, were dictated on the alphabet board.

During the early 1930's Baba's travels began to reach into Europe and then on to America. Contacting literally thousands on both continents, his name rapidly became known to those deeply and sincerely interested in the spiritual disciplines. Some of these he selected into small groups, arranging for them to come later to India. Their visits ranged generally from weeks to years, but before and during World War II all but a small handful were sent back to their homes.

After the war his own travels resumed, but visits of Westerners to India were now normally individual and brief. An exception was the great East-West gathering of November 1962. Thousands of his devotees from all over the world converged on Poona by ship, plane and special trains. For almost a week Baba gave unstintingly of himself in mass darshans, group meetings and personal interviews. The fare was as varied as the assemblage: brief discourses, give and take with old friends, song in praise of God, prayers, embracing the close ones, a day of mass darshan and crowds storming the gates at sunset. The world's literature contains many references to the need for transfusion between East and West. Here was a rich human stew of contrasting elements in which mutual respect, affection and unity in praise of the Loved One bridged vast differences in tradition.

A persistent theme throughout the five decades of Meher Baba's ministration has been his seeking out of the God-intoxicated and his homage to those lamed by disease and want. He has described most clearly through Dr. William Donkin in *The Wayfarers* the difference between those who have lost touch with creation through insanity and those who have merely turned the focus of their hearts to their vision of God. These latter he terms *masts*. Especially in the 1940's, Meher Baba contacted hundreds of these God-intoxicated souls throughout India, often tending personally to their most intimate needs, giving each what only he might know to be required, and returning them finally to their natural surroundings.

Those stricken by leprosy have been a constant concern of Baba. With infinite care and love he washes their feet, bows his forehead to the often twisted stumps on which they hobble, and sends them on their way with renewed hope and peace. "They are like beautiful birds caught in an ugly cage," he once said on such an occasion. "Of all the tasks I have to perform, this touches me most deeply."

While Baba has travelled widely and contacted millions of people, he emphasizes that he has come not to teach, but to awaken. He states that Truth has been given by the great Messengers of the past, and that the present task of humanity is to *realize* the teaching embodied in each of the great Ways. Baba's mission is to awaken man to that realization through the age-old message of love.

Baba also provides the ready example when one is faced by a puzzling decision. In essence, however, one does not know how Baba achieves the results he so clearly elicits from the human instrument. All that the individual senses is a powerful force sweeping through the snarls of life, simplifying and freeing the inner being in a manner that he instinctively trusts.

One of the great wonders of contact with Baba is acceptance. "He invites people to look at themselves, to accept their egotistic selves not as good or bad, clever or stupid, successful or unsuccessful, but as illusions of their true selves, and to cease to identify themselves with the illusion."

The history of man's search for his soul has produced few works dealing with the technique for the soul's discovery. Meher Baba's *Discourses* are a major contribution to that small body of literature. In this work, given to his close disciples in the period 1938–1943, he describes the means for incorporating daily life into one's spiritual ongoing. He also outlines the structure of Creation, but only to clarify the relationship of the aspirant to the Master. In his classic later work, *God Speaks*,* Meher Baba describes in detail the vertical system of God, His will to know Himself consciously, and the purpose of Creation in that will-to-consciousness. The *Discourses* on the other hand are the practical guide for the aspirant as he slowly finds his way back to Oneness, after having developed consciousness through the deeps of evolution.

While the *Discourses* provide detailed descriptions of the Path and its disciplines, the reader will discover

---

*Dodd, Mead and Co., New York, N. Y. 1955; 2nd Revised Ed., 1973.

that they are in no way a do-it-yourself manual for spiritual evolution. Rather, they are a constant, firm reminder of the need for a Master on this Path of apparent return to Oneness. The Master is the knowing guide who has already traversed the Path, who provides with infinite patience the security and steady pace that can lead to the goal. While Baba admits the possibility of achieving progress without such a guide, he makes it clear that it is fraught with almost insurmountable problems.

To one who debates allying himself with a teacher of the inner processes, the *Discourses* provide invaluable insight. To one who senses that life is to be lived for its positive contribution to the discovery of the inner being, Baba provides the unarguable description of one who knows.

"These discourses cover a wide field, but they begin and end with the reader himself. This is therefore a dangerous book. Baba is dangerous, as all who have been near him know . . . . Baba invites those who listen to him to do the impossible because only the impossible has divine meaning."

Meher Baba lives quietly in the midst of the greatest activity, often raising an almost impenetrable barrier to guard the seclusion in which he performs his universal work, near Ahmednagar. On occasion he allows individuals and small groups to penetrate the barrier to receive the spark of love, more rarely he opens the gates wide and loosens a broad river of warmth on those who are lucky enough to know that the Avatar is in the world.

Ivy Oneita Duce
Don E. Stevens
Editors

MEHER BABA

Meher Baba dropped his body on January 31, 1969. The final years of his physical presence were spent in close seclusion marked by painfully intense and exhausting preoccupation with his universal work. In 1968 he announced this had been completed to his 100 percent satisfaction. The same period also witnessed the prairie-fire growth in numbers of those who looked to him for the key to meaning in life. Thousands of these passed before the well-loved form as it lay for seven days in the tomb at Meherabad near Ahmednagar, India. More thousands from all over the world attended the April-to-June darshan he had arranged months before. The impact of these occasions on the inner man, and of the months that have now gone by, bear witness to the force of love set in motion by the one we have known and accepted to be the Avatar of our time.

VOLUME II
CONTENTS

The Search for God

MOST persons do not even suspect the existence of God and naturally they are not very keen about God. There are others who, through the influence of

Grades of beliefs in God

tradition, belong to some faith or another and catch the belief in the existence of God from their surroundings. Their faith is just strong enough to keep them bound to certain rituals, ceremonies or beliefs and rarely possesses that vitality which is necessary to bring about a radical change in one's entire attitude towards life. There are still others who are philosophically minded and have an inclination to believe in the existence of God either because of their own speculations or because of the assertions of others. For them, God is at best an hypothesis or an intellectual idea. Such lukewarm belief in itself can never be sufficient incentive for launching upon a serious search for God. Such persons do not know of God from personal knowledge, and for them God is not an object of intense desire or endeavour.

A true aspirant is not content with knowledge of spiritual realities based on hearsay, nor is he satisfied with pure inferential knowledge. For him the spiritual realities are not the object of idle thinking, and the acceptance or rejection of these realities is fraught with

**True aspirant seeks
direct knowledge of
spiritual realities**

momentous implications for his inner life. Hence he naturally insists upon direct knowledge about them. This may be illustrated from the life of a great sage. One day he was discussing spiritual topics with a friend who was quite advanced upon the Path. While they were engaged in this discussion their attention was diverted to a dead body which was being carried past them. "This is the end of the body but not of the soul," the friend remarked. "Have you seen the soul?" asked the sage. "No," the friend answered. The sage remained sceptical about the soul, for he insisted upon *personal* knowledge.

Although the aspirant cannot be content with secondhand knowledge or mere guesses, he does not close his mind to the possibility that there could be

**Aspirant has an
open mind**

spiritual realities which had not come within his experience. In other words, *he is conscious of the limitations of his own individual experience and refrains from making it the measure of all possibilities.* He has an open mind towards all things which are beyond the scope of his experience. While he does not accept them on hearsay, he also does not rush to deny them. The limitation of experience often tends to restrict the scope of imagination, and thus a person comes to believe that there are no realities other than those which may have come within the ken of his past experience; but usually some incidents or happenings in his own life will cause him to break out of his dogmatic enclosure and become really open-minded.

This stage of transition may also be illustrated by a story from the life of the same sage, who happened to be a prince. Some days after the incident mentioned above, as he was riding on horse-back he came upon

An illustrative story a pedestrian advancing towards him. Since the way of the horse was blocked by the presence of the pedestrian, the sage arrogantly ordered the man out of the way. The pedestrian refused, so the sage dismounted and the following conversation was held: "Who are you?" asked the pedestrian. "I am the Prince," answered the sage. "But I do not *know* you to be the Prince," said the pedestrian and continued, "I shall accept you as a Prince only when I know you to be a Prince and not otherwise." This encounter awakened the sage to the fact that God *may* exist even though he did not know Him from personal experience, just as he was actually a Prince although the pedestrian did not know it from his own personal experience. Now that his mind was open to the possible existence of God, he set himself to the task of deciding that question in earnest.

God either exists or does not exist. *If He exists, search for Him is amply justified. And if He does not exist, there is nothing to lose by seeking Him.* But man does not usually turn to a real search for God as a matter of voluntary and joyous enterprise. He has to be driven to this search by disillusionment with those worldly things which allure him and from which he cannot deflect his mind. Ordinary man is completely engrossed in his activities in the gross world. He lives through its manifold experiences of joys and sorrows without even suspecting the existence of a deeper Reality. He tries as best he can to have pleasures of the senses and to avoid different kinds of suffering.

Ordinary man indifferent to existence of God

"Eat, drink and be merry" is his philosophy, but in spite of his unceasing search for pleasure he cannot altogether avoid suffering, and even when he suc-

**Occasions which
provoke thought**

ceeds in having pleasures of the senses he is often satiated by them. While he thus goes through the daily round of varied experiences, there often arises some occasion when he begins to ask himself, "*What is the end of all this?*" Such a thought may arise from some untoward happening for which the person is not mentally prepared. It may be the frustration of some confident expectation, or it may be an important change in his situation demanding radical readjustment and the giving up of established ways of thought and conduct. Usually such an occasion arises from the frustration of some deep craving. If a deep craving happens to meet an *impasse* so that there is not the slightest chance of its ever being fulfilled, the psyche receives such a shock that it can no longer accept the type of life which may have been accepted hitherto without question.

Under such circumstances a person may be driven to utter desperation, and if the tremendous power which is generated by the psychic disturbance remains

**Unharnessed desper-
ateness is destruc-
tive; divine desperate-
ness is creative**

uncontrolled and undirected, it may even lead to serious mental derangement or attempts to commit suicide. Such a catastrophe overcomes those in whom desperateness is allied with thoughtlessness, for they allow impulse to have free and full sway. The unharnessed power of desperateness can only work destruction. The desperateness of a thoughtful person under similar circumstances is altogether different in results because the energy which it releases is intelligently harnessed and directed towards a purpose. In the moment of such *divine desperateness* a man makes the important decision to discover and realise the aim of life. There thus comes into existence a true search for lasting values. Henceforth the burning query which refuses to be silenced is, "*What does it all lead to* ?"

When the psychic energy of a man is thus centred upon discovering the goal of life, he uses the power of desperateness creatively. He can no longer be content

Divine desperateness is the beginning of spiritual awakening

with the fleeting things of this life and he is thoroughly sceptical about the ordinary values which he had so far accepted without doubt. His only desire is to find the Truth at any cost and he does not rest satisfied with anything short of the Truth. *Divine desperateness is the beginning of spiritual awakening because it gives rise to aspiration for God-realisation.* In the moment of divine desperateness, when everything seems to give way, man decides to take any risk to ascertain what of significance to his life lies *behind* the veil.

All the usual solaces have failed him, but at the same time his inner voice refuses to reconcile itself completely with the position that life is devoid of all meaning.

God or nothing

If he does not posit some hidden reality which he has not hitherto known, then there is nothing at all worth living for. For him there are only two alternatives: either there is a hidden spiritual reality which prophets have described as God, or everything is meaningless. The second alternative is utterly unacceptable to the whole of man's personality, so he must try the first alternative. Thus man turns to God when he is at bay in worldly affairs.

Now since there is no *direct* access to this hidden reality which he posits, he inspects his usual experiences for possible avenues leading to a *significant beyond*. Thus he goes back to his usual experiences with the purpose of gathering some light on the Path. This involves

**Revaluation of experi-
ence in light of posited
Divinity**

looking at everything from a new angle of vision and entails a reinterpretation of each experience. He now not only *has* experience but tries to *fathom its spiritual significance*. He is not merely concerned with what it *is* but with what it *means* in the march towards this hidden goal of existence. All this careful revaluation of experience results in his gaining an insight which could not come to him before he begins his new search.

Revaluation of an experience amounts to a new bit of wisdom, and each addition to spiritual wisdom necessarily brings about a modification of one's general attitude towards

**New insight means
experimenting with
perceived values**

life. So the purely intellectual search for God or the hidden spiritual reality, has its reverberations in the practical life of a man. His life now becomes a real experiment with perceived spiritual values.

The more he carries on this intelligent and purposive experimentation with his own life the deeper becomes his comprehension of the true meaning of life,

**Finding God is com-
ing to one's Self**

until finally he discovers that as he is undergoing a complete transformation of his psychic being he is arriving at a true perception of the real significance of life *as it is*. With a clear and tranquil vision of the real nature and worth of life he realises that *God Whom he has been so desperately seeking is no stranger nor hidden and foreign entity.* He is *Reality itself and not a hypothesis.* He is Reality seen with undimmed vision— that very Reality of which he is a part and in which he has had his entire being and with which he is in fact identical. So, *though he begins by seeking something utterly new, he really arrives at a new understanding of an ancient thing.* The spiritual journey does not consist in arriving at a new destination where a person gains what he did not have, or becomes what he was not. It consists in the dissipation of his ignorance concerning himself and life and the gradual growth of that understanding which begins with spiritual awakening. *The finding of God is a coming to one's own Self.*

The Stages of the Path

ALL persons have to pass through the state of bondage but this period of bondage is not to be looked upon as a meaningless episode in the evolution of life.

Bondage adds to value of freedom

One has to experience being caged if one is to appreciate freedom. If in the entire span of its life the fish has not come out of the water even once, it has no chance of appreciating the value of water. From its birth till its death it has lived only in water, and it is not in a position to understand what water really means to its being. But if it is taken out of water even for a moment, it longs for water and becomes qualified by that experience to appreciate the importance of water. In the same way, if life had been constantly free and manifested no bondage man would have missed the real significance of freedom. *To experience spiritual bondage and know intense desire to be free from it are both a preparation for the full enjoyment of the freedom which is to come.*

As the fish which is taken out of water longs to go back in the water, the aspirant who has perceived the goal longs to be united with God. In fact, the long-

Path begins with longing for deeper reality

ing to go back to the source is present in *each* being from the very time that it is separated from the source by the veil of ignorance, but the being is unconscious of the longing till the aspirant enters the Path. One can in a sense become accustomed to ignorance, just as a person in a train may get accustomed to the darkness of a tunnel when the train has been passing through it for some time. Even then there is a definite discomfort and a vague and undefinable sense of restlessness owing to the feeling that *something* is missing. This something is apprehended from the very beginning as being of tremendous significance. In the stages of dense ignorance, this something is often inadvertently identified with the variegated things of this mundane world. When one's experience of this world is sufficiently mature, however, the repeated disillusionments in life set the man on the right track to discover what is missing. From that moment he seeks a *reality which is deeper than changing forms.* This moment might aptly be described as the first initiation of the aspirant. From the moment of initiation into the Path, the longing to unite with the source from which he has been separated becomes *articulate* and *intense.* Just as the person in the tunnel longs for light all the more intensely after he sees a streak of light coming from the other end, so the person who has had a glimpse of the goal longs to hasten towards it with all the speed he can command.

On the spiritual Path there are six stations, the seventh station being the terminus or the goal. Each intermediate station is, in its own way, a kind of *imaginative anticipation of the goal.* The veil which separates man from God consists of **Wearing out of manifold veil of ignorance** false imagination, and this veil has many folds. Before entering the Path the man is shrouded in this veil of manifold imagination with the result that he cannot even entertain the thought of being other than a separate, enclosed, finite individual. The ego-consciousness has crystallised out of the working of the manifold false imagination, and the conscious longing for union with God is the first shaking of the entire structure of the ego which has been built during the period of the false working of imagination. *Traversing the spiritual Path consists in undoing the results of false working of imagination or dropping several folds of the veil which has created a sense of unassailable separateness and irredeemable isolation.* So far, the man had clung firmly to the idea of his separate existence and secured it behind the formidable walls of thick ignorance, but from now on he enters into some kind of *communication with the larger Reality*. The more he communes with Reality the thinner becomes the veil of ignorance. With the gradual wearing out of separateness and egoism he gains an increasing sense of merging in the larger Reality.

The building up of a sense of aloofness is a result of flights of imagination. Therefore the breaking through of the self-created sense of aloofness and being united with Reality is secured

Gradual reversing of false working of imagination

through reversing the false working of imagination. The act of getting rid of imagination altogether may be compared with the act of awakening from deep *sleep*. The different stages in the process of getting rid of false imagination might be compared with the *dreams* which often serve as a bridge between deep sleep and full wakefulness. The process of getting rid of the manifold working of false imagination is gradual and has seven stages. The shedding of one fold of the veil of imagination is decidedly an advance towards Light and Truth, but it does not amount to becoming one with Reality. It merely means renouncing the more false imagination in favour of the less false imagination. There are different degrees of falseness of imagination corresponding to the degrees of the sense of aloofness constituted by ego-consciousness. *Each stage in the process of getting rid of false imagination is a definite wearing out of the ego.* But all intermediate stages on the Path, until final realisation of the goal, consist in *leaving one flight of imagination for another.* They do not amount to *cessation* of imagination.

These flights of imagination do not bring about any real change in the true being of the Self as it is. *What changes is not the Self but its idea of what it is.* Suppose in a

Intermediate stages on the Path are all forms of imagination

day-dream or phantasy you imagine yourself to be in China while your body is actually in India. When the phantasy comes to an end you realise that your body is actually not in China but in India. From the subjective point of view, this is like returning from China to India. In the same way, gradual non-identification with the body and progressive identification with the Oversoul is comparable with the actual traversing of the *Path*, though in fact the different intermediate stages on the Path are all equally creations of the play of imagination.

The six stages of ascending are thus all within the domain of imagination, but at each stage, *breaking down the sense of aloofness, and discovering a merging in the larger*

Pseudo-sense of realisation

Reality, are both so strong and clear that the person often has a pseudo-sense of realisation. Just as when a person who wants to climb a mountain comes upon a deep valley and is so fascinated by the sight of it that he forgets the real goal and believes for the time being that he has arrived at his goal, so the aspirant also mistakes the intermediate stages for the goal itself. But a person who is really in earnest about climbing the mountain realises after awhile that the valley has to be crossed, and the aspirant also realises sooner or later that the intermediate stage has to be transcended. *The pseudo-sense of realisation which comes at the intermediate stages is like a man's dreaming that he has awakened from sleep althought he is actually still asleep.* After becoming awake he realises that his first feeling of awakening was really a dream.

Each definite stage of advancement represents a state of consciousness, and advancement from one state of consciousness to another proceeds side by side with crossing the inner planes. Thus **Planes and states** six intermediate planes and states of consciousness have to be experienced before reaching the seventh plane which is the end of the journey and where there is final realisation of the God-state. A plane is comparable to a railway *station* where a train halts for some time, and the state of consciousness is comparable to the *movements* of the passenger after getting down at the station.

After entering a new plane of consciousness a person usually takes some time before he can freely function on that plane. As there is a radical change in the total conditions of mental life, **Nature of *Samadhi*** the person experiences a sort of paralysis of mental activity known as *Samadhi* (*Istighraq*). When the pilgrim enters a new plane he merges into that plane before he can experience the state which is characteristic of that plane. Just as a pilgrim who is tired by the strain of the journey sometimes goes to sleep, consciousness which has made the effort of ascending to a new plane goes through a period of *lowered* *mental activity comparable to sleep.* However, *Samadhi* is fundamentally different from sleep, *in that a person is totally unconscious in sleep whereas in Samadhi he is conscious of bliss or light or power, although he is unconscious of his body and surroundings.* After a period of comparative stillness the mind begins to *function* on the new plane and experiences a state of consciousness which is utterly different from the state which it has left behind.

When the aspirant enters a new plane he is merged into it and along with the lowering down of mental activity he experiences a substantial diminution in the ego-life. This curtailment of the ego-life is different from the final annihilation of the ego, which takes place at the seventh plane. But like the

Each stage on path is a curtailment of ego-life

final annihilation at the seventh plane, the different stages of the curtailment of the ego at the intermediate six planes deserve special mention owing to their relative importance. In the Sufi spiritual tradition, the final annihilation of the ego is described as "*Fana-Fillah,*" and the earlier *Samadhi* of the six planes of duality have also been recognised as kinds of *Fana*, since they also involve a *partial* annihilation of the ego.

Through all these Fanas of ascending order there is continuity of progression towards the final Fana-Fillah, and each has some special characteristic. When the pilgrim arrives at the first plane he experiences his first *Fana* or *minor annihilation of the ego.* The pilgrim is temporarily lost to his limited individuality and experiences bliss. Many pilgrims thus merged think they have realised God and hence get stuck in the first plane. If the pilgrim keeps himself free from self-delusion or comes to realise that his attainment is really a transitional phase in his journey, he advances further on the spiritual Path and ar-

First three *Fanas*

rives at the second plane. The merging into the second plane is called *"Fana-e-Batili"* or *the annihilation of the false*. The pilgrim is now absorbed in bliss and infinite light. Some think that they have attained the goal and get stranded in the second plane, but others who keep themselves free from self-delusion march onwards and enter the third plane. The merging into the third plane is called *"Fana-e-Zaheri"* or *the annihilation of the apparent*. Here the pilgrim loses all consciousness of the body or the world for days and experiences infinite power. Since he has no consciousness of the world he has *no occasion for the expression of this power*. This is *Videha Samadhi* or the state of *divine coma*. Consciousness is now completely withdrawn from the entire world.

If the pilgrim advances still further he arrives at the fourth plane. The merging into the fourth plane is called *"Fana-e-Malakuti"* or *the annihilation leading towards freedom*. The pilgrim experi-

Dangers of fourth plane

ences a peculiar state of consciousness at the fourth plane since he now not only *feels* infinite power but also has plenty of occasion for the *expression* of that power. Further, he not only has occasion for the use of his powers but has a definite inclination to express them. If he falls a prey to this temptation he goes on expressing these powers and gets caught up in the alluring possibilities of the fourth plane. For this reason the fourth plane is one of the most difficult and dangerous to cross. The pilgrim is never spiritually safe and his reversion is always possible until he has successfully crossed the fourth plane and arrived at the fifth.

The merging into the fifth plane is called *"Fana-e-Jabaruti"* or *the annihilation of all desires*. Here the incessant activity of the lower intellect comes to a stand-still. The pilgrim does not "think" in the ordinary

***Fanas* of fifth and sixth plane** way, and yet he is indirectly a source of many inspiring thoughts. He sees, but not with the physical eyes. Mind speaks with mind and there is neither worry nor doubt. He is now spiritually safe and beyond the possibility of a downfall; and yet many a pilgrim on this exalted plane finds it difficult to resist the delusion that he has attained Godhood. In his self-delusion he thinks and says, "I am God," and believes himself to have arrived at the end of the spiritual Path. But if he moves on, he perceives his mistake and advances to the sixth plane. The merging into the sixth plane is called *"Fana-e-Mahabubi"* or *the annihilation of the self in the Beloved.* Now the pilgrim sees God directly and clearly as an ordinary person sees the different things of this world. This continual perception and enjoyment of God does not suffer a break even for an instant. Yet the wayfarer does not become one with God the Infinite.

If the pilgrim ascends to the seventh plane he experiences the *last merging* which is called *"Fana-Fillah"* or *the final annihilation of the self in God.* Through this

***Fana-Fillah* or *Nirvi- kalpa Samadhi* a state of conscious Godhood** merging the pilgrim loses his separate existence and be- comes permanently united with God. He is now *one with God* and experiences himself as being none other than God. This seventh plane *Fana-Fillah* is the terminus of the spiritual Path, the goal of all search and endeav- our. It is the *Sahaj Samadhi* or the *Nirvikalpa Samadhi* which is characteristic of *conscious Godhood.* It is the only real awakening. The pilgrim has now reached the opposite shore of the vast ocean of imagination, and realises that *this last Truth is the only Truth* and that all the other stages on the Path are entirely illusory. He has arrived at his final destination.

Arriving at Self-Knowledge

WHEN the time is ripe the advancement of a person towards self-knowledge comes about as naturally as the physical body of the child grows into full-fledged form. The growth of the physical body is worked out by the operation of natural laws, and the progress of the aspirant towards self-knowledge is worked out by the operation of spiritual laws pertaining to the transformation and emancipation of consciousness. The physical body of the child grows very gradually and almost imperceptibly, and the same is true of the spiritual progress of the person who has once entered the Path. The child does not know how its physical body grows; in the same way the aspirant also is often oblivious of the law by which he makes headway towards the destination of his spiritual progress. The aspirant is generally conscious of the manner in which he has been responding to the diverse situations in life, and rarely conscious of the manner in which he makes progress towards self-knowledge. *Without consciously knowing it, the aspirant is gradually arriving at self-knowledge by traversing the Inner Path through his joys and sorrows, his happiness and suffering, his successes and failures, his efforts and rest, and through his moments of clear perception and harmonised will as*

Progress towards Self-knowledge gradual and imperceptible

well as through the moments of confusion and conflict. These are the manifestations of the diverse *sanskaras* which he has brought from the past, and the aspirant forges his way towards self-knowledge through the tangles of these *sanskaras* like the traveller threading his way through a wild and thick forest.

Human consciousness might be compared to the *flash-light* which reveals the existence and the nature of things. The *province* illuminated by this flashlight is

Scope of conscious-ness and its working

defined by the *medium* through which it works, just as a person who is confined to a boat can wander anywhere on the surface of water but can have no access to the remote places on land or in the air. The actual *working* of the flashlight is determined by the accumulated *sanskaras*, just as the course of the rivulets flowing from a mountain is given by the channels created by the natural contours of the mountain.

In the case of an average man, the sphere of life and the stage of action are restricted to the gross world because in him the flashlight of consciousness falls on

Average man only conscious of gross world

the physical body and works through it. Being restricted to the medium of the gross body he can be conscious of anything within the gross world but is unable to establish conscious contact with subtle or mental realities. The gross sphere thus constitutes the arena of the average man, and all his activities and thoughts have a tendency to be directed towards the gross objects which are accessible to him. But all the time he remains unconscious of the subtle and the mental spheres of existence since the flashlight of his consciousness cannot be focussed through the medium of the subtle or the mental body.

At this stage *the soul is conscious of the gross world, but is completely ignorant of its own true nature. It identifies itself with the gross body on which the flashlight of consciousness*

Identification with physical body

falls and this naturally becomes the base for all the activities which are within its range. The soul does not directly know itself through itself but by means of the physical body; and since all the knowledge which it can gather through the physical body points to the physical body itself as the centre of activities, it knows itself as being the physical body which in fact is only its instrument. The soul therefore imagines itself to be man or woman, young or old, and takes upon itself the changes and limitations of the body.

After several rounds of lives in the setting given by the gross world, the impressions connected with the gross world become weak through the *long duration of*

Identification with subtle body

the experience of opposites, like great happiness and intense suffering. The weakening of the impressions is the beginning of the spiritual awakening which consists in the gradual *withdrawal* of the flashlight of consciousness from the allurements of the gross world. When this happens the gross impressions become subtle, facilitating and inducing *the soul's transference of the base of conscious functioning from the gross body to the subtle body.* Now the flashlight of consciousness falls on the subtle body and works through it as its medium, no longer working through the gross body. Therefore the whole gross world drops from the consciousness of the soul and it becomes conscious only of the subtle world. The subtle sphere of existence now constitutes the context of its life and *the soul now considers itself to be the subtle body* which becomes and is seen to be the centre of all its activities. Even when the

soul has thus become subtle-conscious it remains ignorant of its own true nature since it cannot know itself
directly through itself but only by means of the subtle
body. However, the change of the stage of action from
the gross to the subtle sphere of existence is of considerable significance, insofar as in the subtle sphere *the
conventional standards of the gross world are replaced by new
standards which are nearer the Truth, and a new mode of life is
rendered possible by the dawning of new powers and a release of
spiritual energy.* Life in the subtle world is only a passing
phase in the spiritual journey and is far from being the
goal; but out of millions of gross-conscious souls a rare
one is capable of becoming subtle-conscious.

Impressions connected with the subtle world get
worn out in turn through some forms of *penance* or *yoga*.
This facilitates and brings about a further withdrawal

**Identification with
mental body**

of consciousness inwardly
whereby the flashlight of consciousness comes to be thrown
on the *mental body* and begins to function through it.
The severance of conscious connection with the subtle
and gross bodies means that the gross and subtle spheres
of existence become completely excluded from the
scope of consciousness. The soul is now conscious of the
mental world which affords *deeper possibilities for spiritual
understanding and clearer perception of the ultimate Truth.* In
this new setting of the mental sphere, the soul enjoys
continuous inspiration, deep insight and unfailing intuition, and it is in *direct contact with spiritual Reality.*
Although it is in direct contact with God, it does not see
itself as God, since it cannot know itself directly through
itself but only through the medium of the individual
mind. It knows itself by means of the individual mind
and *considers itself to be the individual mind* since it sees the
individual mind as being the base and the centre of all

its activities. Although the soul is now much closer to God than in the gross or subtle spheres, it is still enclosed in the world of shadow and it continues to feel separate from God owing to the veil created by the impressions connected with the mental sphere. The flashlight of consciousness is functioning through the limitation of the individual mind and does not therefore yield the knowledge of the soul *as it is in itself.* Though the soul has not yet realised itself as being God, its life in the mental sphere of existence constitutes a tremendous advance beyond the stage of the subtle sphere. Out of millions of subtle-conscious souls a rare one can establish conscious contact with the mental sphere of existence.

It is possible for an aspirant to rise up to the mental sphere of existence through his own unaided efforts, but *dropping the mental body amounts to the surrenderance of individual existence: This last and all-important step cannot be taken except through the help of a Perfect Master who is himself God-realised.* Out of millions of souls who are conscious of the mental sphere, a rare one can withdraw the flashlight of consciousness from the individual mind. Such withdrawal implies the complete vanishing of the last traces of the impressions connected with the mental life of the soul. When the flashlight of consciousness is no longer centred upon any of the three bodies, it serves the purpose of reflecting the *true* nature of the soul.

Need for a Master

The soul now has direct knowledge of itself without being dependent upon any medium, seeing itself not as some finite body but as infinite God, and knowing itself to be the only Reality.

Direct Self-knowledge

This major crisis in the life of the soul is conditioned by the complete *severance of connection with all three bodies.* Since consciousness of the different spheres of existence is directly dependent upon corresponding bodies, the soul is now entirely *oblivious of the whole universe*. The flashlight of consciousness is no longer focussed upon anything foreign or external but is turned upon the soul itself. The soul is now truly Self-conscious and has arrived at Self-knowledge.

The process of arriving at Self-knowledge throughout the three spheres of existence is attended by *the acquisition of false self-knowledge consisting in identification*

False self-knowledge a temporary substitute for true self-knowledge

with the gross or the subtle or the mental body, according to the stage of the process. This is due to the initial purpose of creation which is to make the soul Self-conscious. The soul cannot have true Self-knowledge except at the end of the spiritual progress, and all the intermediate forms of false self-knowledge are, as it were, *temporary substitutes for true Self-knowledge*. They are *mistakes necessary* to the attempt to arrive at true Self-knowledge. Since the flashlight of consciousness is turned throughout the journey towards the objects of the environment and not upon the soul itself, the soul has a tendency to become so engrossed in these objects that it is almost completely oblivious of its own existence and nature. *This danger of utter and unrelieved self-forgetfulness is counterbalanced by the self-affirmation of the soul by means of the body, which happens to be used as the focal point of the flashlight of consciousness.* Thus the soul knows itself as its own body and knows other souls as their bodies, thereby *sustaining a world of duality where there is sex, competition, aggression, jealousy, mutual fear and self-centred exclusive ambition.* Self-knowledge of the soul by means of a *sign* is a source of untold confusion, complication and entanglement.

This form of ignorance may be illustrated by

means of the famous *pumpkin* story referred to by the poet Jami in one of his couplets. Once upon a time

Story of the pumpkin

there was an absent-minded man who had no equal in forgetting things. He had an intelligent and trusted friend who wanted to help him to remember himself. This friend attached a pumpkin to his neck and said, "Now listen, old man, one day you might completely lose yourself and not know who you are. Therefore, as a *sign* I tie this pumpkin around your neck, so that every morning when you wake up you will see the pumpkin and know that you are there." Every day the absent-minded man saw the pumpkin after waking up in the morning and said to himself, "*I am not lost.*" After some time, when the absent-minded man had become used to self-identification through the pumpkin, the friend asked a stranger to remain with the absent-minded man, take away the pumpkin from his neck during his sleep and tie it around his own neck. The stranger did this, and when the absent-minded man woke up in the morning, he did not see the pumpkin around his neck. So he said to himself, "*I am lost.*" He saw the pumpkin on the other man's neck and said to him, "*You are me. But then who am I?*"

This *pumpkin* story offers an analogy to the different forms of *false* self-knowledge growing from identification with the body. To know oneself as the body is like

Analogy made explicit

knowing oneself by means of the pumpkin. The disturbance caused by non-identification with the gross, subtle or mental body is comparable to the confusion of the absent-minded man when he could no longer see the pumpkin around his own neck. The beginnings of a dissolution of the sense of duality are equivalent to the absent-minded man's identification of himself as the stranger who wore his pumpkin. Further, if the absent-minded man in the story were to learn to know himself through himself independently of any external sign, his self-knowledge would be comparable to the true Self-knowledge of the soul which, after ceasing to identify with the three bodies, knows itself to be none other than infinite God. *Arriving at such Self-knowledge is the very goal of creation.*

God-Realisation

TO arrive at true self-knowledge is to arrive at God-realisation. God-realisation is a unique state of consciousness. It is different from all the other states of consciousness because all the

To realise the Self is to realise God

other states of consciousness are experienced through the medium of the individual mind; whereas the state of God-consciousness is in no way dependent upon the individual mind or any other medium. *A medium is necessary for knowing something other than one's own self. For knowing one's own self no medium is necessary.* In fact, the association of consciousness with the mind is definitely a hindrance rather than a help for the attainment of realisation. The individual mind is the seat of the ego or the consciousness of being isolated. It creates the limited individuality, which at once feeds on and is fed by the illusion of duality, time and change. So, in order to know the Self as it is, consciousness has to be completely freed from the limitation of the individual mind. In other words, the individual mind has to disappear but consciousness has to be retained.

·Throughout the past life-history of the soul, its consciousness has grown with the individual mind and all the workings of consciousness have proceeded against the background of the individual mind. *Consci-*

Consciousness inter-twined with the mind *ousness has therefore come to be firmly embedded in the individual mind* and cannot be extricated from this setting into which it has been woven. The result is that if the mind is suborned, consciousness also disappears. The intertwining of the individual mind and consciousness is amply illustrated by the tendency to become unconscious when there is any effort to stop mental activity through meditation.

The everyday phenomenon of going to sleep is not essentially different from the lull experienced during meditation, but it is slightly different in its *origin.*

Explanation of sleep Since the individual mind is continuously confronted by the world of duality it is involved in ceaseless conflict; and *when it is wearied by its unrelieved struggle, it wants to lose its identity as a separate entity and go back to the Infinite.* It then recedes from the world of its own creation and experiences a lull, and this lull is also invariably accompanied by the cessation of consciousness.

The quiescence of mental activity in sleep entails the complete submerging of consciousness; but this cessation of mental life and conscious functioning is only temporary, because *the*

Resuming wakeful-ness *impressions which are stored in the mind goad it to renewed activity.* After awhile the psychic stimuli of impressions result in stirring the mind and reviving the conscious functioning which is performed through its medium. So the period of sleep is followed by a period of wakefulness and the period of wakefulness is followed by a period of sleep, according to the law of alternating activity and rest. As long as the latent impressions in the mind are not completely undone, however, there is no final annihilation of the individual mind or emancipation of consciousness. In sleep the mind temporarily forgets its identity but it does not finally lose its individual existence. When the person awakens he finds himself subject to his old limitations. There is a resurrection of consciousness, but it is still mind-ridden.

The limited mind is the soil in which the ego is securely rooted, and this ego perpetuates ignorance through the many illusions in which it is caught. The ego prevents manifestation of infinite knowledge which is already latent in the soul; it is the most formidable obstacle to the attainment of God. A Persian poem says truly, "It is extremely difficult to pierce through the veil of ignorance; for there is a rock on the fire." Just as a flame cannot rise very high if a rock is placed upon it, a desire to know one's own true nature cannot lead to the Truth as long as the burden of the ego is placed on consciousness. *Success in finding oneself is rendered impossible by the continuation of the ego which persists throughout the journey of the soul.* In old age, an aching tooth can give untold trouble because it is not easily uprooted, although moving within its socket. In the same way the ego which might become feeble through love or penance, is yet difficult to eradicate. It persists till the very end. Though it becomes looser as the soul advances on the Path, it remains till the last stage which is the seventh plane.

Obstacle of the ego

Ego is the centre of all human activity. The attempts of the ego to secure its own extinction might be compared to the attempt of a man to stand on his own shoulders. Just as the eye cannot see itself, so the ego is unable to end its own existence. All that it does to bring about self-annihilation only goes to add to its own existence. *It flourishes on the*

Difficulty of over-coming the ego

very efforts directed against itself. Thus it is unable to vanish altogether through its own desperate activity, although it succeeds in transforming its own nature. The disappearance of the ego is conditioned by the melting away of the limited mind which is its seat.

The problem of God-realisation is the problem of emancipating consciousness from the limitations of the mind. When the individual mind is dissolved, the whole universe which is relative to the mind vanishes into noth-ingness, and consciousness is

Parallel between sleep and God-realisation

no longer tied to anything. Consciousness is now unlimited and unclouded by anything and serves the purpose of illumining the state of the Infinite Reality. While immersed in the bliss of realisation the soul is completely oblivious of sights or sounds or objects in the universe. In this respect it is *like sound sleep*, but there are many important points of difference which distinguish God-realisation from sound sleep. During sleep the illusion of the universe vanishes, since all consciousness is in abeyance, but there is no conscious experience of God, since this requires the complete dissolution of the ego and the turning of full consciousness towards the Ultimate Reality. Occasionally, when the continuity of deep sleep is interrupted by brief intervals, the soul may have the experience of retaining consciousness without being conscious of anything in particular. There is consciousness; but this consciousness is not of the universe. It is consciousness of *nothing*. Such experiences anticipate God-realisation in which consciousness is completely freed from the illusion of the universe and manifests the infinite knowledge which was hitherto hidden by the ego.

In sleep, the individual mind continues to exist,

although it has forgotten everything including itself; and the latent impressions in the mind create a veil be-

Difference between sleep and God-realisation

tween the submerged consciousness and the Infinite Reality. Thus, *during sleep, consciousness is submerged in the shell of the individual mind, but it has not yet been able to escape from that shell.* So, though the soul has forgotten its separateness from God and has actually attained unity with Him, it is unconscious of this unity. *In God-realisation, however, the mind does not merely forget itself but has (with all its impressions) actually lost its identity.* The consciousness which was hitherto associated with the individual mind is now freed and untrammeled and brought into direct contact and unity with the Ultimate Reality. Since there is now no veil between consciousness and the Ultimate Reality, consciousness is fused with the Absolute and eternally abides in It as an inseparable aspect promoting an unending state of infinite knowledge and unlimited bliss.

The manifestation of infinite knowledge and unlimited bliss in consciousness is, however, strictly confined to the soul which has attained God-realisation.

God-realisation is personal

The infinite Reality in the God-realised soul has explicit knowledge of its own infinity; but such explicit knowledge is not had by the unrealised soul, which is still subject to the illusion of the universe. Thus if God-realisation were not a personal attainment of the soul, the entire universe would come to an end as soon as any one soul achieved God-realisation. This does not happen, because *God-realisation is a personal state of consciousness belonging to the soul which has transcended the domain of the mind.* Other souls continue to remain in bondage and though they also are bound to receive God-realisation one day they can only attain it by freeing their consciousness from the burden of the ego and the limitations of the individual mind. Hence the attainment of God-realisation has a direct significance only for the soul which has emerged out of the time-process.

After the attainment of God-realisation, *the soul discovers that it has always been the Infinite Reality which it now knows itself to be*, and that its regarding itself as finite

What was latent in the Infinite becomes manifest

during the period of evolution and spiritual advancement was in fact an illusion. The soul also finds out that the infinite knowledge and bliss which it now enjoys have also been latent in the Infinite Reality from the very beginning of time and that they merely became manifest at the moment of realisation. Thus the God-realised person does not actually become something different from what he was before realisation. He remains what he was, and the only difference which realisation makes in him is that *previously he did not consciously know his own true nature, and now he knows it*. He knows that he has never been anything other than what he now knows himself to be and that what he has been through was but a *process of finding himself*.

The whole process of attaining God-realisation is just a *game in which the beginning and the end are identical*. The attainment of realisation is nevertheless a distinct

Two types of advantages

gain for the soul. There are two types of advantages: one consists in *getting what one did not previously possess*, the other in *realising fully what one really is*. God-realisation is of the second type. However, this creates an infinite difference between the soul which has God-realisation and the soul which does not have

God-realisation. Though the God-realised soul does not possess anything new, its explicit knowledge of all that it really is, has been and will ever be, makes God-realisation all-important. The soul which is not God-realised experiences itself as being finite and is constantly troubled by the opposites of fleeting joys and sorrows; but the soul which has realisation is lifted out of them and experiences *the infinite knowledge and the unlimited bliss of being God-conscious.*

In God-realisation the soul drops its separate consciousness and transcends duality in the abiding knowledge of its identity with the Infinite Reality. *The shackles*

Value of God-realisation *of limited individuality are broken; the world of shadows is at an end; the curtain of illusion is forever drawn. The feverishness and the agonising distress of the pursuits of limited consciousness are replaced by the tranquility and bliss of Truth-consciousness. The restlessness and fury of temporal existence are swallowed up in the peace and stillness of Eternity.*

True Discipleship

WHEN an aspirant becomes voluntarily affiliated with a Master, he is said to have become a disciple. But if this affiliation is merely formal, it does not
Discipleship is vital relation
constitute true discipleship. The relationship between disciple and Master is *utterly different from the legal relations which create rights and liabilities through verbal transactions or formal agreements*. Discipleship is one of the fundamental features which characterise the life of the advanced aspirant, and it does not come into existence through any artificial procedure. It *arises out of the basic laws of spiritual life*. It is therefore much more significant than the mundane relations which arise within the context of ordinary social life as a result of incidental associations or temporary contracts. Many of these mundane relations do not enter into the spiritual fabric of the life of the aspirant but remain superficially attached to his being. Thus it is not of any great consequence whether you purchase a thing from one shop-keeper or another as long as you pay the price for it; and it is immaterial whether you travel by one ship or another so long as you arrive at your destination. Even such transactions are no doubt inwardly determined by *sanskaric* ties and *karmic* laws, and therefore are not entirely devoid of spiritual significance. But

these relations are in their very nature provisional and superficial, and are in no way comparable to the vital bond of discipleship which *gives substance and direction to the life of the aspirant.*

The relation between Master and disciple is an inevitable outcome of intrinsic conditions in the life of the aspirant. It is primarily a relation between the lover and his Divine

Love implied in discipleship is unique

Beloved. From the spiritual point of view it is the most important relationship into which a person can enter. The love which constitutes the core of discipleship stands by itself among the different types of love which prevail in ordinary social relations. Mundane love is an interplay between two centres of God-unconscious; but *the love implied in discipleship is the love of God-unconscious for God-conscious.* Everyone is God, but some are unconscious of their divinity, some are partly conscious of their divinity and a few are fully God-conscious. Those who are unconscious of their divinity can have no idea of the God-state; they are only conscious of the body-state. In order that they should inherit the God-state they have to love, worship and be guided by the Master who is constantly dwelling in the God-state.

The love which the aspirant has for the Master is really the response evoked by the greater love which the Master has for the aspirant. It is to be placed *above all*

Supremacy of claim of the Master

other loves. Love for the Master naturally becomes a central power in the life of the aspirant because he knows the Master to be an embodiment and representation of Infinite God. All his thoughts and aspirations, therefore, come to be woven around the personality of the Master. The Master thus has unquestioned supremacy among the claims recognised by the aspirant, and *it is through this supremacy that the Master be-comes the focal point for the radiation of spiritual forces* which dispel all darkness, pluck out the sins of the heart and initiate the aspirant into a life of freedom and Truth-consciousness.

The fundamental requisite for the candidate who would be a true disciple is an unquestioning love for the Master. *All the other streams of love ultimately join this great river of love for the Master and disappear in it.* Majnu loved

All love leads to the Master

Laila. He loved her so intense-ly that every moment of his life he was filled with thoughts about her. He could not eat, drink or sleep without thinking of her; and all he wanted was the hap-piness of Laila. He would gladly have seen her married to some other person if he felt it to be in her interest, and he would even have died for her husband if he had thought she would thereby be happy. The utter self-denial and sincerity of his love ultimately led him to the Master. Every second of his life he thought not of himself but of the beloved, and this lifted his love from the physical or intellectual level and made it spiritual. The spiritualisation of his love led him to the Divine Beloved.

The Master is the Divine Beloved, and when the disciple meets his Master, all that he has to do is to love him; for if the disciple loves the Master out of the full-ness of his heart, his final union with him is assured. He need not worry about the quality of his love. He should love in spite of his weaknesses and not tarry till he can purify his own heart. The Master is the very source of purity, and *to set one's heart on the Master is the beginning of self-purification.* When the disci-ple has whole-hearted devotion for the Master, he opens

Purification through love and self-surrender

himself to the reception of the divine love which the Master pours upon him. All his weaknesses are consumed in this fire of divine love of which he thus becomes the recipient. If the disciple is to be free from all weaknesses and attain incorruptible and infinite purity, he has to *dedicate his life to the Master without any reservations or provisions.* He must offer his weaknesses as well as his vices, his merits as well as his sins. There should be no "if's" and "but's" about his offering. His self-surrender must be so complete as to allow no room in his mind for even a shadow of any secret self desire.

Complete self-surrender and unquestioning love become possible when the disciple achieves unswerving faith in the Master. *Faith in the Master is an indispensable part of true discipleship.* Once

Value of faith

God is realised there is no question of faith at all, just as there is no question of faith when a man knows himself to be a man. But till this state of realisation is attained, the faith which the disciple places in the Master is his most reliable guiding light and is comparable to the steering wheel of the ship. *It is not correct to describe faith as being blind, for it is more like sight than like unrelieved ignorance,* but it has to be short of direct experience until the aspirant realises God for himself. It is not for nothing that all the religions are referred to as "faiths." One of the essentials of the aspirant's life is that he should have faith. Faith may express itself through diverse forms, but from the psychological point of view they are one and the same thing and cannot be diversely labelled. The only differences in faith are differences of degree. Faith may be strong and vital, or weak and lukewarm. A weak and lukewarm faith does not carry a man further than adherence to rituals and ceremonies, but *a strong and vital faith is bound to take the aspirant beyond the external forms of religion* and help him to eschew the husk and get at the kernel of true spiritual life. *Faith reaches its natural climax and goal when it comes to rest in one's own Master.*

The faith of the disciple must always be securely grounded in his experience of the divinity of the Master. He must not be like a straw carried anywhere by the slightest breeze. He should be

Story of Kalyan

like a rock which remains un-moved in the severest of storms. The story of Kalyan brings out the meaning of a really sound faith in the Master. Kalyan was a disciple of Swami Ramdas who was a Perfect Master at the time of Shivaji.

The Master loves all disciples alike, but some might be particularly dear to him, just as a man loves all parts of his body, but the eyes may be more dear to him than his fingers.

Swami Ramdas had many disciples, but his favourite was Kalyan. Other disciples did not quite understand why Kalyan should be dearer to the Master than the others. Once Swami Ramdas tested the devotion of his disciples. He asked all his disciples to come to him and pretended to be so sick as to be on the point of death. He had placed a mango on the joint of his knee and bound it up by means of a bandage so that it looked like a huge swelling. Swami Ramdas pointed to this swelling and told the disciples that it was a malignant tumour and that there was no chance of his living unless someone sucked the poison from the joint of his knee. At the same time he made it clear to all that whoever sucked out the poison would die instanta-neously. Then he asked whether any disciple was prepared to suck out the poison from the swelling at the cost of life. All the disciples hesitated except Kalyan who arose immediately and began to suck from the swelling. To his surprise Kalyan found sweet mango juice and not poison and Swami Ramdas praised his unswerving faith and self-denying love. To be willing to die for the happiness of the Beloved is true love. Such implicit faith, unfaltering love and undivided loyalty as that of Kalyan can come to the disciple only through the grace of the Master.

Undivided loyalty to the Master does not introduce any narrowness in the sphere of the disciple's life. To serve the Master is to serve your own self in every other self. The Master dwells in universal consciousness and wills universal spiritual well-being.

The Master realised through service

To serve the Master is therefore to participate in his cause, which is to serve all life. While sharing in the work of the Master, the disciple may be required to be in touch with the world; but, though moving in the world in accordance with the work which is in store for him, he is in inward contact with the Master as Infinite Being. Therefore, *by sharing in the work of the Master the disciple comes closer to him and becomes an integral part of his consciousness*. Serving the Master is the quickest means of realising him.

The service which the disciple can offer the Master is not only linked with the universal cause of humanity but is one of the most potent means of bringing the disciple nearer his spiritual goal. When the disciple's service is spontaneous, whole-hearted, selfless and unconditional it brings him more spiritual benefit than can ever come by any other means.

Sharing work of the Master

Serving the Master is a joy for the disciple even when it means an ordeal that tries his body or mind. Service offered under conditions of discomfort or inconvenience is a test of the disciple's devotion. The more trying such service becomes, the more welcome it is for the disciple, and as he voluntarily accepts physical and mental suffering in his devoted service to the Master, he experiences the bliss of spiritual fulfillment.

The sense of undivided and absolute loyalty to the Master is made possible by the right understanding of what the Master is and what he really stands for. If the disciple has an imperfect grasp of the true status and function

Cases of conflict

of the Master, he is likely to set up a *false antithesis* between his own higher Self and the Master. As a consequence of this antithesis he might create in his mind an artifical and imaginary conflict between the claims of the Master and other claims which seem legitimate. A disciple should realise from the very beginning the Master only requires that the disciple should realise his own higher Self. In fact, *the Master symbolises this higher Self of the disciple and is none other than this higher Self which is the same one reality in all.* So, allegiance to the Master is only another form of allegiance to one's higher Self. This does not mean, however, that merely formal allegiance to the higher Self is in any way an adequate substitute for allegiance to the Master. *The disciple cannot have a clear perception of his own higher Self until he is God-realised and often that which comes to him as his duty is really a prompting of some sanskaras interpolating themselves between the higher Self and his field of consciousness.* The Master on the contrary is one with the higher Self and can make no mistake about right valuation.

The disciple therefore must always test his own promptings by means of the standards or orders given by the Master, and in the event of any conflict between the two, he should thoroughly re-examine his own ideas to

Cases of conflict

discover the points wherein they might be short of perfection. Almost always a little reflection is sufficient to
complete his own thinking and to perceive the *basic
harmony between the true dictates of his own higher Self and
the requirements of the Master.* If, however, on some rare
occasion the disciple is unable to reconcile the two, he
may be sure that he has either not properly understood
the dictates of his own higher Self or that he has not
properly grasped the import of his Master. In such cases
the Master himself requires that the disciple should follow his own conscience at any cost. The Master may
sometimes give instructions with the intent of preparing
his disciple for a higher mode of life, and it is under such
circumstances that the disciple finds himself confronted
by an apparent and temporary variance between his
own inclinations and the Master's instructions. But
usually the Master does not give any instructions for
which the disciple has not had inward anticipatory
preparation.

The Master is supremely impersonal and always
his only concern is to remove the veils between the
consciousness of the disciple and his higher Self. There-

**Real meaning of
discipleship**

fore there can never be any
real conflict between the allegiance of the disciple to his
Master and his allegiance to his own higher Self. Indeed, at the end of his search, *the disciple discovers that the
Master is none other than his own Higher Self in another form.*
The Master in his utter impersonality and unhampered
divinity is so complete that he has no desire. In relation
to the disciple all that he requires is that the disciple
should reconstitute himself in the light of the highest
Truth. To become a disciple is to begin to tread the
Path leading towards the spiritual goal. This is the
meaning of true discipleship.

The Ways of the Masters

MASTERS are absolutely impersonal and universal in their consciousness, but for spiritual purposes they can limit the scope of their work and also allow

Masters ever ready to help

their manifested personality to become the centre of the aspirations of their disciples. *They use personal relationships as well-defined channels to pass on their help to those aspirants who become connected with them.* The Masters are always on the lookout for those who need and deserve their help and the faintest gleams of spiritual yearnings are not overlooked by them. They foster and promote the advancement of all aspirants in multifarious ways which are unfailingly effective, although they might not necessarily be completely intelligible to others.

The help of the Master consists in making the spiritual journey of the aspirant sure and safe as well as in shortening the time which he might otherwise

Nature of their help

take for arriving at the goal. The aspirant may go a long way through independent search, but he in unable to cross the sixth plane without the help of a Master. Even on the intermediate planes the help of the Master is extremely valuable, because he *prevents the aspirant from getting stuck on the way and protects him from the pitfalls and dangers with which the spiritual Path is beset.* Kabir has compared the three stages of the Path to the three phases of fire. Just as first there is only smoke and no fire, then there is fire enveloped in smoke, and lastly there is only fire without smoke, the beginnings of the Path are enveloped in thick ignorance, midway there is confused perception of the goal, and finally there is realisation of Truth without the slightest alloy of illusion. Since the Path lies through illusions of many kinds, the aspirant is never safe without the guidance of the Master who knows all the stages of the Path and can take him through them.

Before the opening of the inner eye the mind conceives of the goal as the Infinite, and this conception is based upon some symbolic image of Infinity such as

Abode of delusion the sky or the ocean, which suggests the idea of vastness. Although such a concept of the Infinite is clean-cut and well defined, it has to be superseded by direct perception of the Infinite. The aspirant sees the Self *directly* when his inner eye of the spirit is opened. When this happens, the mind is dazed by what it sees and is no longer as clear as it was before the opening of this inner eye. Being dazed by the perception of the Self, the mind loses its capacity to think clearly and mistakes the seeing of the Self with its being actually realised. Hence comes the illusion of being at the end of the Path when one is still traversing it. In *Sufi* terms this particular part of the Path is known as *Mukam-e-afasan* or the *Abode of Delusion*. It is in such difficult phases of the Path that the Master can, through his skillful intervention, give a push to the aspirant so that he keeps on going instead of getting caught up on the way.

In fact, there is danger of the aspirant being detained on each one of the inner planes, because each in its own way is very alluring and serves as a trap for the aspirant. The Master either takes the aspirant past these planes or through them without unnecessary delay. *The aspirant has to walk his own way, but the contribution of the Master consists in confirming and consolidating the previously acquired intuitions and perceptions of the aspirant, and in precipitating his consciousness into the next stage* which, though unavoidable, is by its nature impossible for him to anticipate.

Contribution of the Master

The Master uses *Maya* to take the disciple out of *Maya*, and as he is himself beyond good and evil he may often require things which are unacceptable and even shocking to the ordinary good sense of his disciples. The best thing for the disciple to do is to follow the instructions of the Master with implicit faith, without bringing them to the bar of his limited capacity of judgment. The following famous instances illustrate this point.

Unquestioning faith of disciples

There is the Koranic story of Abraham being called upon to sacrifice his beloved son Ismael to the Lord. When Abraham, firm in his resolve and faith, was about to slaughter his son and Abraham's knife was already pointing at his throat, Ismael was miraculously saved by being replaced by a goat.

Shams-e-Tabriz ordered Maulana Rumi, his disciple, to fetch wine for him from a pub, which he unflinchingly complied with in order to please and win the grace of his Master. At the time Maulana commanded a large following of Muslim divines on account of his reputation as a great theologian of the Islamic world, and wine is religiously prohibited (*Haram*) to the Muslims. Hence it was a crucial test for Maulana to carry a jar of wine on his shoulders through the streets, but he did it.

Ghousali Shah was asked by one of his Masters, who lived in a hut by the side of the river Ganges, to get a vessel full of water only from mid-stream, for drinking. It was about midnight and the river Ganges was in heavy flood because of the monsoon. The disciple hesitated at first but finally gathered courage to attempt the impossible, believing in the omniscience of the Master. No sooner had he stepped into the angry waters of the Ganges than he witnessed a wonderful transformation of the scene. Instead of the surging waves and the floods, the river had turned into a thin stream and the vessel to be filled almost touched the river bed. The disciple nearly crossed the river to the opposite bank in search of the mid-stream. While thus occupied, the Master appeared on the scene and asked him the reason for his delay. When Ghousali explained that the mid-current could not be located, the Master allowed him to fill the vessel by handfuls and himself helped in the process. The Master then left the disciple on some pretext, asking him to follow immediately after filling the vessel. When Ghousali Shah returned to the hut with the vessel full of water, he was bewildered to learn from other disciples that the Master had never left the hut for a minute during his absence, but was talking to them all the while about him.

These stories show how the Master may use his occult powers on rare occasions to break down the ego of his disciples or help them further on the Path. *As a rule the Masters are very sparing in the use of their divine powers,* and they never use them *unless it is absolutely necessary for spiritual purposes.* Ordinarily they secure their purposes through *normal mundane ways.* While doing so they not

Masters usually prefer ordinary to occult methods

only exhibit great understanding, keen sense of humour, unending patience and consummate tact, but they also take great trouble to help their disciples, and adjust themselves in numberless ways to whatever might be entailed by the needs of the situation.

Some of these points are effectively brought out by the story of the great mystic Bahlul. Bahlul wanted to contact certain notables of Persia for reasons of his

Story of Bahlul

own. The only way to do this was to go to the Prince's party which was attended by these notables. Unfortunately Bahlul was bald-headed, and in those days no one without hair was allowed to attend a party given by the Prince. The Prince had lost all his hair, and to see others without hair reminded him of it and prevented him from enjoying the party. Since the Prince was very sensitive on this point, no bald person was allowed to come to the party, so when Bahlul, who was bald, went to the party in his shabby clothes, he was thrown out. The party lasted for three days, however, and on the second day Bahlul borrowed some fine clothes and a wig, disguised himself and again went to the party.

During the party no one recognised Bahlul, and in his fine clothes he made a great impression upon all the notables. He made himself so agreeable that even the Prince offered him a warm welcome and invited him to sit near him. No sooner was Bahlul seated than he winked at the Prince. The Prince did not understand the meaning of his winking but vaguely felt that such a gesture from an illustrious man like him must mean something important. Thinking that it immediately required a suitable response, he also winked. Those who were nearby saw this exchange of winking and felt impelled to imitate them. They also winked at each other, and soon the winking spread throughout the crowd so that for five minutes the party saw nothing but winking. Then Bahlul cried, "Stop! O you wise men. Why do you wink?" And the notables replied, "We are winking because you great men were winking. We only imitate you." Then immediately Bahlul took off his wig and said, "We two are both bald. Imitate us." The notables then went away and on the third day they all came with shaved heads. Then Bahlul turned to the Prince and said, "We two are permanently bald; these men will have to shave their heads daily in order to remain bald." Thus through his tactful handling and sense of humor he secured access to those whom he wanted to help.

The Master takes infinite pains to contact and win over the disciple for spiritual life. Since the progress of the disciple is secured only if his love for the

Dealing with failings of disciples

Master is not allowed to dwindle, he takes every care to remove all obstacles which might be standing in the way of the whole-hearted devotion of the disciple. *If sometimes he is seen to humour the individual nature of the disciple it is only to keep those obstacles from creating a serious impediment in his way.* Sometimes he might even seem to feed the ego of the disciple, but all this is just giving a long rope to the ignorance of the disciple. It is only a preparation for the final extinguishing of his ego, just as animals to be offered in sacrifice are carefully nurtured before their annihilation. The Master is himself beyond good or evil and is not perturbed by the failings of the disciple. He tolerates them with unfailing patience and infinite capacity to wait, knowing full well that once the disciple gets established on the Path these failings will be swiftly washed away.

Once the Master is satisfied that the disciple is

firmly established in the Path, he is keen to cleanse the mind of the disciple of all blemishes. Often he achieves this task even at the risk of appearing ruthless, just as when a surgeon, completely disregarding the protests of the patient, is active with his knife. Ultimately the disciple cannot fail to see that all such measures are really in his interest. Therefore he is never weaned away from his Master but is drawn closer to him in the very process of cleansing which might have appeared irksome or painful.

The usual method of the Master, however, is as sweet and agreeable for the disciple as it is effective. The Master is very pleased when the disciple shows any real progress in

Help through praise

the spiritual line. *By conferring well-merited praise on the disciple he confirms in him the spiritual qualities which he is in process of realising and arouses in him the confidence which will enable him to cope with any situation.* The glow of noble emotion, a gesture of self-denial, a heroic sacrifice or an incident revealing extraordinary patience or love or faith—any one of these is sufficient to make the Master happy and evoke his approbation. The usual method of the Master to encourage the good qualities in the disciple is plain and unconcealed appreciation of his attainments. The disciple soon begins to value the Master's approval and delights in it more than in anything else. He is ready to resist the greatest of temptations and undergo the most trying ordeals, which would otherwise have seemed impossible to him, if only he knows that this will make the Master happy.

Since the Master is, for the aspirant, a symbol of the supreme Self in all, the problem of true adjustment

Solution of all problems

to the Master appears to him to be the same as realising his own inner divinity and arriving at true adjustment with all other forms of the Supreme Self. Through his allegiance to the Master the aspirant gives effect to his conscious appreciation of the fundamental unity of all these problems. *From the psychological point of view he is in a position to tackle them not as separate problems but as aspects of one problem. Thus he can arrive at true integration, which is different from a temporary compromise between conflicting claims.* In order to help the disciple to achieve this difficult task the Master has to become *the nucleus of all the spiritual idealism of the aspirant,* because intensive concentration of psychic energy is necessary if the aspirant is to break through the many barriers which lie between him and his goal.

The supremacy of claim which the Master has cannot be challenged or limited even by the spontaneous reverence which the disciple is bound to feel for Masters

Imperative claim of the Master

other than the one who has accepted him. All Perfect Masters are *one* in their consciousness and it is absurd to imagine any grades between them. Though one Master is not greater than another, the disciple must, for his own purposes, place the claim of his own Master over and above the claims of other Masters until he transcends the domain of duality and realises the unity of all life. *Psychic energy would be dissipated unless there arose a supremely imperative claim among the many conflicting claims of life.* Exclusive concentration upon one Master is therefore usually indispensable for the gathering up of the dispersed psychic energy of the disciple. In very rare cases, owing to special circumstances, the Masters themselves might decide to share the spiritual work in relation to a particular disciple. There are, therefore, exceptional cases of disciples who have had to affiliate themselves to two or more Masters. This is an *exception* rather than the rule, and *where there are more Masters than one, they arrange the distribution of their work so carefully that they do not set up any conflict of claims.*

The Nature of the Ego
and its Termination

PART I

THE EGO AS THE CENTRE OF CONFLICT

IN the pre-human stage consciousness *has* experiences, but these experiences are not explicitly brought into relation with a central "I." The dog is angry, but he

Origin of the ego

does not continue to feel, "I am angry." Even in his case we find that he learns through some experiences and thus bases the action of one experience on another, but this action is a result of a semi-mechanical tension of connected imprints or *sanskaras*. It is different from the intelligent synthesis of experiences which the development of I-consciousness makes possible. *The first step in submitting the working of isolated impressions to intelligent regulation consists in bringing them all into relation with the centre of consciousness which appears as the explicit limited ego.* The consolidation of the ego-consciousness is most clear and defined from the beginning of human consciousness.

Human consciousness would have been nothing more than a repository for the accumulated imprints

Process of ego-formation

of varied experiences, if it had not also contained the principle of ego-centred integration, which expresses itself in the attempt to organise and understand experience. The process of understanding experience implies capacity to hold different bits of experiences together as parts of a unity and the capacity to evaluate them by being brought into mutual relation. *The integration of the opposites of experience is a condition of emancipating consciousness from the thraldom of diverse compulsions and repulsions which tend to dominate consciousness irrespective of valuation. The early attempts to secure such integration are made through the formation of the ego as its base and centre.*

The ego emerges as an explicit and unfailing accompaniment to all the happenings of mental life in order to fulfill a certain need. The part played by the ego in human life may be compared to the function of *ballast in a ship*. The ballast in a ship keeps it from oscillating too much. Without it the ship is likely to be too light and unsteady and is in danger of being overturned by the lawless winds. The psychic energy would be caught up endlessly in the multitudinous mazes of dual experience and would all be frittered away and dissipated if there were no *provisional nucleus* to take stock of all acquired experience and bind together the active tendencies born of the relatively independent and loose instincts inherited from animal-consciousness. *The formation of the ego serves the purpose of giving a certain amount of stability to conscious processes and also secures a working equilibrium which makes for a planned and organised life.*

Ego arises to fulfill a need

It would be a mistake therefore to imagine that the arising of the ego is without any purpose. Though it arises only to vanish in the end, it does temporarily fulfill a need which could not have been ignored in the long

Necessary evil

journey of the soul. The ego is not meant to be a permanent handicap, since it can be transcended and outgrown through spiritual endeavour; but the phase of ego-formation must nevertheless be looked upon as a *necessary evil*, which has to come into existence for the time being.

The ego thus marks and fulfills a certain necessity in the further progress of consciousness. But since *the ego takes shelter in the false idea of being the body*, it is a

Ego-centred integration based on illusion

source of much illusion which vitiates experience. *It is of the essence of the ego that it should feel separate from the rest of life by contrasting itself with other forms of life.* Thus, though inwardly trying to complete and integrate individual experience, the ego also creates an artificial *division between external and internal life* in the very attempt to feel and secure its own existence. This division in the totality of life cannot but have its reverberations in the inner individual life over which the ego presides as a guiding genius.

While always striving to establish unity and integration in experience, the ego can never realise this objective. Though it establishes a certain kind of

Ego becomes a seat of conflicts

balance, this balance is only provisional and temporary. *The incompleteness of its attainments is evident from the internal conflict which is never absent as long as experience is being faced from the point of view of the ego.* From moment to moment the mind of man is passing through a series of conflicts. The minds of great and distinguished persons as well as the minds of common people are seen to be harassed by conflicting desires and tendencies. Sometimes the conflict with which the mind is faced is so acute that the person concerned yields to the psychic pressure and there is either a partial or total derangement of mind. There is really no vital difference between the normal man and the so-called abnormal man. *Both have to face the same problems, but the one can more or less successfully solve his problems and the other cannot solve them.*

The ego attempts to solve its inner conflicts through false valuation and wrong choice. *It is characteristic of the ego that it takes all that is unimportant as important and all that is important as unimportant.* Thus power, fame, wealth, ability and other worldly attainments and accomplishments are really unimportant, but the ego takes delight in these possessions and clings to them as "mine." On the other hand, true spirituality is all-important for the soul, but the ego looks upon it as unimportant. For example, if a person experiences some bodily or mental discomfort while doing a work of spiritual importance, the ego steps in to secure the unimportant bodily or mental comfort even at the cost of giving up the really important spiritual work. Bodily and mental comfort, as well as other worldly attainments and accomplishments, are often necessary, but they are not therefore important. *There is a world of difference between necessity and importance.* Many things come to the ego as being necessary, but they are not in themselves important. Spirituality, which comes to the ego as being unnecessary, is really important for the soul. The ego thus represents a deep and fundamental principle of ignorance which is exhibited in *always preferring the unimportant to the important.*

Ego attempts to solve conflicts through false valuation

The mind rarely functions harmoniously because it is mostly guided and governed by forces in the subconscious, and few persons take the trouble to attain mastery over these hidden forces which direct the

Conflict can be solved through true valuation

course of mental life. *The elimination of conflict is possible only through conscious control over the psychic forces in the sub-conscious;* and this control can be permanently attained only through the repeated exercise of true valuation in all the cases of conflict which are presented to the mind.

If the mind is to be freed from conflict it must always make the right choice and must unfailingly prefer the truly important to the unimportant. *The*

Need for intelligent choice

choice has to be both intelligent and firm in all cases of conflict— important as well as unimportant.

It has to be intelligent, because only through the pursuit of true and permanent values is it possible to attain a poise which is not detrimental to the dynamic and creative flow of mental life. An unintelligent choice, if it is stern, may temporarily overcome conflict, but it is bound in the long run to curtail the scope of life or to hamper the fulfillment of the whole personality. Moreover, the conflict will surely reappear in some other form if it has not been intelligently solved. An intelligent solution, on the other hand, requires an insight into true values, which have to be disentangled from false values. The problem of the conflict of desires thus turns out to be the problem of conflicting values, and *the solution of mental conflict therefore requires a deep search for the real meaning of life.* It is only through wisdom that the mind can be freed from conflict.

Having once known what the right choice is, the next step is to stick to it firmly. Although the competing tendencies in the mind may be quieted by choosing

Fidelity to right choice

one particular course in preference to other alternatives, they still continue to act as obstacles in making the choice fully effective and operative. At times there is a danger of a decision being subverted through the intensification of those competing psychic forces. To avoid defeat the mind must stick tenaciously to the right value which it has seen. Thus *the solution of mental conflict requires not only perception of right values but also an unswerving fidelity to them.*

The intelligent and firm choice, however, has to be repeatedly exercised in *all* matters—small or great— for *the ordinary "worries" of life are not in any way less important than the serious "problems"*

True valuation must govern all matters *with which the mind is confronted in times of crisis.* The roots of mental conflict cannot completely disappear as long as there is only intermittent exercise of intelligent and firm choice. The life of true values can be spontaneous only when the mind has developed the unbroken habit of choosing the right value. Three-quarters of our life is made up of ordinary things, and though conflict concerning ordinary things may not cause mental agony, it still leaves in the mind a sense of uneasiness that something is wrong. The conflicts which turn upon ordinary things are rarely even brought to the surface of consciousness. Instead they cast a shadow on one's general feeling about life as if from behind a screen. *Such conflicts have to be brought to the surface of consciousness and frankly faced before they can be adequately solved.*

The process of bringing conflict to the surface of consciousness should not degenerate however into a process of imagining conflict where there is none. *The*

Hidden conflicts *sure sign of a real hidden conflict is the sense that the whole of one's heart is not in the thought or action which happens to be dominant at the moment.* There is a vague feeling of a narrowing down or a radical restriction of life. On such occasion an attempt should be made to analyse the mental state through deep introspection, for such analysis brings to light the hidden conflicts concerning the matter.

When the conflicts are thus brought to light it is possible to resolve them through intelligent and firm choice. The most important requirement for the satis-

The ideal as motive-power

factory resolution of conflict is motive power or inspiration, which can only come from a burning longing for some comprehensive ideal. Analysis in itself may aid choice, but *choice will remain a barren and ineffective intellectual preference unless it is vitalised by zeal for some ideal appealing to the deepest and most significant strata of human personality.* Modern psychology has done much to reveal the sources of conflict, but it has yet to discover methods of awakening inspiration or supplying the mind with something which makes life worth living. This indeed is the creative task facing the saviours of humanity.

The establishment of the true ideal is a beginning of right valuation. Right valuation in turn is the un-doing of the constructions of the ego, which thrives on

Disintegration of ego-centre through right valuation

false valuation. *Any action which expresses the true values of life contributes towards the disintegra-tion of the ego, which is a product of ages of ignorant action.* Life cannot be permanently imprisoned within the cage of the ego. It must at some time strive towards the Truth. In the ripeness of evolu-tion comes the momentous discovery that *life cannot be understood and lived fully as long as it is made to move round the pivot of the ego.* Man is then driven by the logic of his own experience *to find the true centre of experience and reorganise his life in the Truth.* This entails the wearing out of the ego and its replacement by Truth-consciousness. The disintegration of the ego culminates in realising the Truth. *The false nucleus of consolidated* sanskaras *must disappear if there is to be a true integration and fulfillment of life.*

The Nature of the Ego
and its Termination

PART II

THE EGO AS AN AFFIRMATION OF SEPARATENESS

THE ego is an affirmation of separateness. It takes
many forms. It may take the form of a continued
self-conscious memory expressing itself in recollections
like, "I did this and I did
that; I felt this and I felt that;
I thought this and I thought
that." It also takes the form of ego-centred hopes for
the future expressing themselves through plans like,
"I shall do this and I shall do that; I shall feel this and
I shall feel that; I shall think this and I shall think
that." Or again in the present, the ego manifests itself
in a strong feeling of being *someone in particular* and as-
serts its distinctness and separateness from all the other
centres of consciousness. While provisionally serving a
useful purpose as a centre of consciousness, *the ego, as
an affirmation of separateness, constitutes the chief hindrance
to spiritual emancipation and enlightenment of consciousness.*

The ego affirms its separateness through craving,
hate, anger, fear or jealousy. When a person craves for
the company of others he is keenly conscious of being
separate from them and thus feels his own separate ex-

**Ego is an affirmation
of separateness**

Ego feeds upon exclusive feelings

istence intensely. The feeling of separation from others is most acute where there is great and unrelieved craving. In hate and anger also the other person is, so to speak, thrown out of one's own being and regarded not only as a foreigner but as definitely hostile to the thriving of the ego. Fear also is a subtle form of affirming separateness and exists where the consciousness of duality is unabated. Fear acts as a thick curtain between the "I" and the "you" and it not only nourishes deep distrust of the other, but inevitably brings about *a shrinking and withdrawal of consciousness so as to exclude the being of another from the context of one's own life.* Therefore, not only other souls but God should be loved and not feared. To fear God or His manifestations is to strengthen duality; to love them is to weaken it.

The feeling of separateness finds most poignant expression in jealousy. There is a deep and imperative need in the human soul to love and identify itself with

Complications of jealousy strengthen ego

other souls. This is not fulfilled in any instance where there is craving or hate, anger or fear. In jealousy, in addition to the non-fulfillment of this deep and imperative need for identification with other persons, there is a belief that some other soul has successfully identified itself with the person whom one sought. This creates a standing and irreconcilable protest against *both* individuals for developing a relationship which one really wished to reserve for oneself. *All exclusive feelings like craving, hate, fear or jealousy bring about a narrowing down of life and contribute to the limitation and restriction of consciousness. They become directly instrumental in the affirmation of separateness and the ego.*

Every thought, feeling or action which springs from the idea of exclusive or separate existence binds. All experiences—small or great—and all aspirations—good or bad—create a load of impressions and nourish the sense of the "I." *The only experience which makes for the slimming down of the ego is the experience of love, and the only aspiration which makes for the alleviation of separateness is the longing to become one with the Beloved.* Craving, hatred, anger, fear and jealousy are all exclusive attitudes which create a gulf between oneself and the rest of life. *Love alone is an inclusive attitude which helps bridge this artificial and self-created gulf, and tends to break through the separative barrier of false imagination.* The lover too longs, but he longs for union with the Beloved. In seeking or experiencing union with the Beloved the sense of the "I" becomes feeble. In love the "I" does not think of self-preservation, just as the moth is not at all afraid of getting burnt in the fire. *The ego is the affirmation of being separate from the other, while love is the affirmation of being one with the other. Hence the ego can be dissolved only through real love.*

Slimming down of ego through love

The ego is implemented by desires of varied types. Failure to fulfill desires is a failure of the ego. Success in attaining desired objects is a success of the ego. *Through the fulfilled desires as well as through the unfulfilled ones the ego is accentuated.* The ego can even feed upon the comparative lull in the surging desires and assert its separative tendency through feeling that it is desireless. *When there is real cessation of all desires, however, there is cessation of the desire to assert separativeness in any form. Therefore real freedom from all desires brings about the end of the ego.* The bundle of the ego is made of faggots of multicoloured desires, and the breaking of these faggots

Ego made of desires

amounts to the destruction of the ego.

The problem of erasing the ego from consciousness is very complicated, however, because the roots of the ego are all in the subconscious mind in the form of latent

Roots of ego in sub-conscious mind

tendencies; and these latent tendencies are not always accessible to explicit consciousness. The limited ego of explicit consciousness is only a small fragment of the total ego. The ego is like an iceberg floating in the sea. About one-seventh of the iceberg remains above the surface of the water and is visible to the onlooker, and the major portion remains submerged and invisible to the onlooker. In the same way, *only a small portion of the real ego becomes manifest in consciousness in the form of an explicit "I," and the major portion of the real ego remains submerged in the dark and inarticulate sanctuaries of the subconscious mind.*

The explicit ego which finds its manifestation in consciousness is by no means a harmonious whole; it can and does become an arena for multitudinous

Ego heterogeneous in constitution

conflicts between opposing tendencies. It has a limited capacity however for allowing simultaneous emergence of conflicting tendencies. Two persons have to be at least on speaking terms if they are to enter into articulate wrangling. If they are not on speaking terms they cannot bring themselves to quarrel on common ground. In the same manner, two tendencies which can enter into conscious conflict must have some common ground. If they are too disparate they cannot find admittance into the arena of consciousness, *even as conflicting tendencies*, but have to remain submerged in the subconscious mind until they are both modified through the tension exerted by the diverse activities connected with the conscious mind.

Although the entire ego is essentially heterogeneous in its constitution, *the explicit ego of consciousness is less heterogeneous than the implicit ego of the subconscious mind. It operates as a formidable whole compared with the isolated subconscious tendencies which seek to emerge in consciousness.* The organised ego of explicit consciousness thus becomes a repressive barrier which indefinitely prevents several constituents of the implicit ego from access to consciousness. All the problems of the ego can be tackled only through intelligent and conscious action, and therefore *complete annihilation of the ego is possible only when all the constituents of the ego pass through the fire of intelligent consciousness.*

Explicit ego and implicit ego

The action of intelligent consciousness on the components of the explicit ego is important, but in itself it is not sufficient for the desired results. The components of the implicit ego of the subconscious mind have to be brought to the surface of consciousness somehow and become parts of the explicit ego, and then be submitted to the action of intelligent consciousness. If this is to be achieved, there has to be a weakening of the explicit ego in such manner as to allow the emergence into consciousness of those desires and tendencies which could not hitherto find admittance into the arena of consciousness. This release of inhibited tendencies naturally brings about additional confusion and conflict in the explicit ego. Therefore the disappearance of the ego is often accompanied by intensified conflicts in the arena of the conscious mind rather than by any comfortable easing of them. However, *at the end of the uncompromising and acute struggle lies the state of true poise*

Intensified conflict a condition of attaining unassailable harmony

and unassailable harmony which comes after the melting away of the entire iceberg of the ego.

The digging out of the buried roots of the ego from the deeper layers of the subconscious and bringing them to the light of consciousness is one important part of the process of wiping out the ego. The other important part consists in the intelligent handling of desires *after* they gain entrance to the arena of consciousness. The process of dealing with the components of explicit consciousness is by no means clear and simple, for the explicit ego has a tendency to live through *any* one of the opposites of experience. If it is ousted from one opposite by the intensive operation of intelligent consciousness, it has a tendency to move to the other extreme and live through it. *Through repeated alternation between the opposites of experience the ego eludes the attack of intelligent consciousness and seeks to perpetuate itself.*

Ego lives through opposites of experience

The ego is hydra-headed and expresses itself in numberless ways. It lives upon *any* type of ignorance. Pride is the specific feeling through which egoism manifests. A person can be proud of most unimportant and silly things. Instances are known of persons developing their nails to an abnormal length and preserving them, despite much inconvenience to themselves, for no other reason than to assert separateness from others. The ego must magnify its attainments in a grotesque manner if it is to live in them. Direct assertion of the ego through self-display in society is very common, but if such direct assertion is prohibited by the rules of decency, the ego has a tendency to seek the same result through the *slander of others*. To portray others as evil is to glorify oneself by *suggesting* a comparison, which

Ego is hydra-headed

the ego would fain develop, but abstains from it for other reasons.

The ego is activated by the principle of *self-perpetuation* and has a tendency to live and grow by any and all means not closed to it. *If the ego faces curtailment in one*

Tricks of the ego

direction it seeks compensating expansion in another. If it is overpowered by a flood of spiritual notions and actions, it even tends to fasten upon this very force which is originally brought into play for the ousting of the ego. If a person attempts to cultivate humility in order to relieve himself of the monstrous weight of the ego and succeeds in doing so, the ego can, with surprising alacrity, *transfer itself to this attribute of humility.* It feeds itself through repeated assertions like "I am spiritual," just as in primary stages it achieved the same task by assertions like "I am not interested in spirituality." Thus arises what we might call a *spiritual ego*, or the ego which feels its separateness through the attainment of things which are considered to be good and highly spiritual. From the truly spiritual point of view, this type of spiritual ego is as binding as the primary and crude ego which makes no such pretensions.

In fact, in the more advanced stages of the Path, the ego does not seek to maintain itself through *open* methods but takes shelter in those very things which

Guerilla warfare

are pursued for the slimming down of the ego. These tactics of the ego are very much like guerilla warfare and are the most difficult to counteract. The ousting of the ego from consciousness is necessarily an intricate process, and cannot be achieved by exercising a constantly uniform approach. Since the nature of the ego is very complicated, an equally complicated treatment is needed to get rid of it. Since the ego has almost infinite possibilities for making its existence secure and creating self-delusion, the aspirant finds it impossible to cope with the endless upcropping of fresh forms of the ego. *He can hope to deal successfully with the deceptive tricks of the ego only through the help and grace of a Perfect Master.*

In most cases it is only when the aspirant is driven to realise the futility of all his efforts that he approaches the Master. By himself he can make no headway towards the goal which he dimly sights and seeks. The stubborn persistence of the ego exasperates him, and *in this clear perception of helplessness he surrenders to the Master as his last and only resort.* The self-surrender amounts to an open admission that the aspirant now has given up all hope of tackling the problems of the ego by himself and that he relies solely upon the Master. It is like saying, "I am unable to end the wretched existence of this ego. I therefore look to you to intervene and slay it." This step, however, turns out to be more fruitful than all other measures which might have been tried for the slimming down and subsequent annihilation of the ego. When, through the grace of the Master, the ignorance which constitutes the ego is dispelled, there is the dawn of Truth which is the goal of all creation.

Master is the last resort

The Nature of the Ego and its Termination

THE ego subsists upon mundane possessions like power, fame, wealth, ability, attainments and accomplishments. It creates and recognises the "thine"

Ego lives through idea of "mine"

in order to feel what is distinctively "mine." However, in spite of all the worldly things which it claims as "mine," it constantly feels empty and incomplete. To make up for this deep restlessness in its own being, it seeks to fortify itself through further acquisitions. It brings the array of its entire varied possessions into relief by comparison with others who might be inferior in any one of the items stamped as "mine" and often uses these possessions for wanton and uncalled for self-display even to the disadvantage of others. The ego is dissatisfied *in spite* of its mundane possessions, but instead of cultivating detachment from them it seeks to derive satisfaction from a more intense sense of possession in contradistinction to others. *The ego as an affirmation of separateness lives through the idea of "mine."*

The ego wants to feel separate and unique and it

seeks self-expression either in the role of someone who is decidedly better than others or in the role of someone

Forms of the ego

who is decidedly inferior. *As long as there is ego, there is an implicit background of duality;* and as long as there is the background of duality, the mental operations of comparison and contrast cannot be effectively stilled forever. Therefore even when a person seems to feel a sense of equality with another, this feeling is not securely established. It marks a point of transition between the two attitudes of the ego rather than permanent freedom from the distinction between the "I" and the "you."

This pseudo-sense of equality, where it exists, may be stated in the formula, "I am not in any way inferior or superior to the other." This will at once be seen to be

Idea of equality

a negative assertion of the ego. The balance between the "I" and the "you" is constantly disturbed by the predominance of a superiority or inferiority complex. The idea of equality arises to restore this lost balance. *The negative assertion of the ego in the form of equality is, however, utterly different from the sense of unity* which is characteristic of the life of spiritual freedom. Although the sense of equality is made the basis of many social and political ideals, *the real conditions of rich co-operative life are fulfilled only when the bare idea of equality is replaced by the realisation of the unity of all life.*

The feelings of superiority and inferiority are reactions to each other, and the artificially induced feeling of equality might be regarded as a reaction to both.

Two complexes

In all these three modes the ego succeeds in asserting its separateness. *The superiority complex and the inferiority complex for the most part remain disconnected from each other.*

They both seek separate and alternate expression through suitable objects, as when a person dominates those whom he regards as his inferiors and submits to those whom he looks upon as his superiors. But such alternative expression through contrasting behaviour only accentuates these opposite complexes instead of leading to their dissolution.

The superiority complex is stirred when a person meets one who is in some way remarkably inferior to him in mundane possessions. *In spite of its many posses-*

Superiority complex *sions the ego is constantly confronted with the spectacle of its intrinsic emptiness. Therefore it clings to the comforting delusion of its worthwhileness by demonstrating the greatness of its possesssions.* This contrast is not confined to theoretical comparison, but often exhibits itself in an actual clash with others. Thus aggressiveness is a natural outcome of the need to compensate for the poverty of the ego-life.

The inferiority complex is stirred when a person meets some one who is in some way remarkably superior to him in respect of mundane possessions. But

Inferiority complex his submissiveness to the other is rooted either in fear or selfishness. It can never be whole-hearted or spontaneous, because there is a lurking jealousy and even hatred for the other for possessing something which he would rather have for himself. All forced and outward submission is purely the effect of an inferiority complex, and can only enhance the ego in one of its worst forms. *The ego attributes its sense of emptiness to the apparently inferior possessions which it can claim as "mine," rather than to the radical viciousness of seeking fulfillment through possessions.* Awareness of its inferiority in possessions becomes only a further stimulus for making desperate efforts to add to its possessions through such means as are available to it. Thus, while perpetuating the inward poverty of the soul, *the inferiority complex, like the superiority complex, constitutes an agent for selfishness and social chaos, and the accumulation of that type of ignorance which characterises the ego.*

When a person comes into contact with the Master and recognises him as having the state of egoless perfection, he voluntarily surrenders himself to the Master,

Surrender utterly different from inferiority complex because he perceives the ego to be a source of perpetual ignorance, restlessness and conflict and also recognises his own inability to terminate it. But this self-surrender should be carefully distinguished from the inferiority complex, because it is accompanied by awareness that the Master is *his* ideal and as such has a basic unity with the disciple. Such self-surrender is in no way an expression of loss of confidence. On the contrary it is an expression of confidence in the final overcoming of all obstacles through the help of the Master. *The appreciation of the divinity of the Master is the manner in which the higher Self of the disciple is expressing its sense of dignity.*

In order to bring about a rapid dissolution of these two chief forms of the ego, the Master may deliberately stir both of these complexes in alternation.

Intervention by the Master If the disciple is on the point of losing heart and giving up the search he might arouse in him deep self-confidence. If he is on the point of becoming egotistic he might break through this new barrier by creating situations in which the disciple has to accept and recognise his own incapacity or futility. Thus *the Master wields his influence over the disciple to expedite the stages through which the melting ego passes before* *its final disappearance.*

The superiority and inferiority complexes have to be brought into intelligent relation with each other if they are to counteract each other. This requires a psy-

Adjustment to the Master involves dissolution of complexes through mutual tension

chic situation in which, for the time being, both will be allowed to have their play at one and the same time, without requiring the repression of the one in order to secure the

expression of the other. When the soul enters into a dynamic and vital relation with the Master, the complexes concerned with the senses of inferiority and superiority are both brought into play and they are so intelligently accommodated that they counteract each other. The disciple feels that he is *nothing in himself,* but in and through the Master he is enlivened by the prospect of being *everything. Thus at one stroke the two complexes are brought into mutual tension, and tend to annihilate each other in the attempt which the disciple makes to adjust himself to the Master.* With the dissolution of these opposite complexes there comes a breaking down of the separative barriers of the ego in all its forms. With the breaking down of the barriers of separation there arises divine love. With the arising of divine love the separate feeling of the "I," as distinguished from "you," is swallowed up in the sense of their unity.

For a car to move towards its destination a driver is necessary. But this driver may be susceptible to strong attachments for things that he encounters on the way, and he might not

Analogy of driver

only halt at intervening places for an indefinite time, but also get lost in the wayside in pursuit of things that have only temporary charm. In that case he might keep the car moving all the time but without coming nearer the goal, and he might even get further away from it. Something like this happens when the ego assumes control of human consciousness. The ego may be compared to a driver who has a certain amount of control over a car and a certain capacity to drive it, but who is in complete darkness about its ultimate destination.

For a car to reach its ultimate destination, it is not enough merely to have a driver who can work and manage the engine. It is equally necessary that this driver should be able to direct the car towards the destination. As long as the movement of consciousness is under the full and exclusive domination of the ego, the spiritual advancement of the person is jeopardised by the natural tendency of the ego to strengthen the separative barriers of false imagination. So, in spite of ego-centred activities, consciousness remains enclosed by the walls of its own creation and moves within the limits of this *mayavic* prison. If consciousness is to be emancipated from its limitations and rendered adequate to serve the original purpose for which it came into existence, *it must draw its directive momentum not from the ego but from some other principle.* In other words, the *driver* who is ignorant of the ultimate destination must be exchanged for another driver who is free from all the allure of accidental things encountered on the way, and who centres his attention not on the rest stations or side-attractions but on the ultimate goal of non-duality. *The shifting of the centre of interest from unimportant things to truly important values is comparable to the transference of power from the ignorant driver to the driver who knows the destination.* Concurrent with this gradual shifting of the centre of interest there is progressive dissolution of the ego and motion towards the Truth.

If the ego had been nothing but a medium for the

integration of human experience it would have been possible for one to get established in the final Truth

Ego attempts integration around false idea

merely by carrying further the activity of the ego. But while playing a specific part in the progress of consciousness, the ego also represents an active principle of ignorance which prevents further spiritual development. *The ego attempts the integration of experience, but it does so around the false idea of separateness. Having taken an illusion as a foundation for the construction of its edifice, it never succeeds in anything but the building of illusions one upon another.* Arriving at the Truth is actually hindered rather than helped by the function of the ego. The process of arriving at the Truth can be fruitful only if *the integration presided over by the ego is carried further without bringing in the basic ignorance of separateness.*

As long as human experience lies within the limitation of duality, integration of experience is an inevitable condition for a rational and significant life. But

Master becomes new nucleus of integration

the ego as a nucleus for integration has to be renounced because of its inevitable alliance with the forces of ignorance. There arises then an imperative need for a *new* centre of integration which will steer clear of the basic ignorance of separateness, and which will allow free scope for the incorporation of all values which were inaccessible to the ego-centre. Such a new centre is provided by the Master who expresses all that has real value, and who represents the absolute Truth. *The shifting of interest from unimportant things to important values is facilitated by allegiance and self-surrender to the Master who becomes the new nucleus for integration.*

The Master, when truly understood, is a standing affirmation of the unity of all life. Allegiance to the Master, there-

fore, brings about a gradual dissociation from the ego-nucleus

Union with Master is the realisation of Truth

which affirms separateness. After this important crisis in the life of man, all mental activity has a new frame of reference, and its significance is to be gathered in the light of its relation to the Master as the manifestation of infinite Truth, not in the light of any relation to the ego-centre as a limited "I." The person henceforth finds that all acts which flow from him are no longer initiated from the limited "I," but are all inspired by the Truth working through the Master. He is also no longer interested in the well-being of the limited self, but is interested in the Master as representing universal and undivided life. He offers all his experiences and desires to the Master, reserving neither the good nor the evil for the limited "I," stripping the ego of all content. This advancing bankruptcy of the ego does not interfere with the process of integration, because the function is now performed around the new centre of the Master as representing the Truth. *When the ego-nucleus is completely bankrupt and devoid of any power or being, the Master as Truth is firmly established in consciousness as its guiding genius and animating principle. This constitutes both the attainment of union with the Master and the realisation of the infinite Truth.*

When the ego gradually adjusts itself to the spiritual requirements of life through the cultivation of humanity, selflessness and love, whole-hearted surrender

Review of evolution

and offering oneself to the Master as truth, it suffers a drastic curtailment. It not only offers less and less resistance to spiritual unfoldment, but also undergoes a radical transformation. This eventually turns out to be so great that in the end the ego, as an affirmation of separateness, completely disappears and is substituted by the Truth which knows no separateness. The intermediate steps of slimming down the ego and softening its nature are comparable to the trimming and pruning of the branches of a wild and mighty tree, while the final step of annihilation of the ego amounts to the complete uprooting of this tree. When the ego disappears entirely there arises knowledge of the true Self. Thus *the long journey of the soul consists in developing from animal consciousness the explicit self-consciousness as a limited "I," then in transcending the state of the limited "I" through the medium of the Master. At this stage the soul is initiated into the consciousness of the supreme and Real Self as an everlasting and infinite "I am" in which there is no separateness, and which includes all existence.*

The Place of Occultism in Spiritual Life

PART I
THE VALUE OF OCCULT EXPERIENCES

SPIRITUAL emancipation of consciousness brings with it an unfoldment of many psychic capacities which are latent in the human soul. This unfoldment increases the scope and range of human consciousness. New elements often play an important part in helping or hindering the spiritual emancipation of consciousness. Therefore, the aspirant not only has to understand the value of such occult experiences as unusual and significant dreams, visions, glimpses of the subtle world and astral journeys, but also has to learn to distinguish such occult realities from hallucinations and delusions.

Psychic capacities help or hinder emancipation

Although it is customary to exaggerate the importance of occult experiences, it is not uncommon to doubt their validity and to treat them with a contempt which is usually accorded to all forms of mental aberrations and abnormalities. *The attitude of unqualified contempt for occult experience is of course most pronounced in those who*

Contempt for occult experiences born of ignorance

are not even abecedarians in direct knowledge of occult realities.
It hurts the ego to admit and feel that there might be
vast unexplored fields of the universe which are accessible just to a limited number of persons, and from
which one happens to be excluded. The undeserved
contempt which occultism at times receives is almost
always the outcome of profound ignorance about
its real meaning. This attitude of contempt is of course
different from a cautious and critical attitude. *Those
who have a cautious and critical approach are endowed with
humility and openness of mind, and are ever ready to recognise
and admit occult realities when they occur.*

The Master usually helps the aspirant through
ordinary means and prefers to take him under the veil,
but when there is a special indication he may also use

**Some dreams spirit-
ually important**

an occult medium to help
him. Special types of dreams
are among the common media
which are used for touching the deeper life of the aspirant. *Masters have not infrequently first contacted aspirants
by appearing in their dreams.* Such dreams, however,
have to be carefully distinguished from ordinary
dreams. In ordinary dreams the subtle body is active
in exercising its functions of seeing, tasting, smelling,
touching and hearing, but the soul is not using the
subtle body with full consciousness. As these experiences of ordinary dreams are received *subconsciously,*
they are in most cases purely *subjective,* relating to
physical activities and concerning gross living, and
are the creations of nascent *sanskaras* stored in the
mind. In some cases, however, a dream which is
indistinguishable from ordinary dreams may be the
reflection in the subconscious of some objective experience of the subtle body, and not merely a product
of fancy.

Most dreams are purely subjective and sub-conscious experiences of the subtle body and they have no special spiritual significance, except that they can

Rare types of dreams be occasions for forging new *sanskaras* or spending up old ones and that occasionally they shed light upon the hidden complexes and unfaced problems of personality. Such dreams can never include something which is not in some way a part of the past experience of the person. They allow scope for novelty only in respect of new combinations of items which have already appeared in past experience. *The rare types of dreams are those about persons and things unknown in this life but known in some past life or lives. Still more rare are the dreams of persons and things which have never appeared in this life or former lives but are going to appear in this life in the future.* Ordinary dreams are thus utterly different from dreams which have occult significance.

Very often, when the aspirant is having psychic unfoldment he has occasional experience of the subtle world in the form of significant visions, lights, colours,

Beginnings of occult experience sounds, smells or contacts. At first these experiences are fitful and the aspirant is likely to treat them as hallucinations. But *even when he treats them as hallucinations, he finds it impossible to resist their directive influence because of their intrinsic potency.* The spiritual journey, however, becomes more smooth if the aspirant learns to cultivate the right attitude, towards occult experiences, which consists in taking them for what they are worth. This balanced attitude is just the thing which the aspirant in the initial stages finds it difficult to maintain.

The beginner is apt to exaggerate the importance of his glimpses into the inner worlds and develop an ungovernable

craving for repetition of these experiences, or he tries to treat

Balanced attitude to occult experience very rare

them as abnormal phenomena and underrates their significance. Of these two alternatives, the attitude of exaggerating the importance of occult experiences is the most common, because the novelty and rarity of occult experiences are the factors which contribute to charging them with overwhelming importance.

In fact, the ego of the aspirant tends to become attached to this new field revealed to him, and gives him the sense of being a rare person admitted to an

Craving for occult experience

exclusive privilege. The more experiences a person has the greater scope he desires. He also develops the habit of depending upon occult goading for each step on the Path, just as those who take drugs get addicted to them and require stimulation even for doing things which they could formerly do without such stimulation. In order to avoid this pitfall for the aspirant, the Master takes good care not to cater to his new craving for occultism. *Occult experiences are vouchsafed to the aspirant if and when they are absolutely necessary for spiritual purposes and not when he wants or asks for them.*

If the aspirant is found to attach undue importance to occult experiences or to develop an ungovernable craving for them, the Master might deal with this

Dealing with craving for occult experience

obstacle in his own way by actually weakening or annulling the occult experiences which have become the basis for false search. This is like giving immediate relief to a patient by surgical removal of the root cause of a physical disorder. It serves the purpose of protecting the aspirant from forging fresh chains for self-limitation. The aspirant must not be allowed under any circumstances to get caught up in false values and wrong search. These can only lead to side-tracking and cause unnecessary delay in achieving the real goal, which is to get initiated into the truly spiritual life. The introduction of the aspirant into occult realities is necessarily a very gradual and prolonged process. The Master is never anxious to expedite it, as *few persons are really qualified to stand the expansion of their experience in this new dimension.*

In the initial stages the appearance of occult realities is very fitful and the aspirant sometimes doubts their claims to validity, treating them with caution in order to rule out the possibility of his being deluded. *But occult experiences often bear unmistakable credentials for their own claim to validity, and even when any such credentials are not evident they compel due respect and attention because of the unusual significance, bliss, peace and directive value with which they are surcharged.* Mainly because of these characteristics, the aspirant is able to distinguish real occult experiences from hallucinations and delusions.

Validity of occult experience

Hallucinations are erroneous perceptions and consist in actually seeing or hearing things which do not really exist. Though they are clearly different in this respect from merely imagining things, they remain objects of doubt in spite of their similarity to normal perceptions. Delusions are even more deceptive because they consist not only in actually seeing things which really do not exist, but also in having complete conviction of their existence. But ordinary hallucinations and delusions do not bring extraordinary

Occult experience must be distinguished from hallucination and delusion

bliss or peace to the person who experiences them. *The bliss and peace which are attendant upon real occult experiences are a fairly reliable criterion by which to distinguish them as genuine.* Hallucinations are like the nightmare of wakeful consciousness.

Even when occult experience can be clearly differentiated from illusion, it is deficient in power and efficacy and subject to poignant doubt. This happens

Beneficiary of occult help must develop self-confidence

when the person who has had the experience discusses the matter with others who, because of their incapacity to understand such things, throw out contrary thoughts and shake his conviction. For this reason, in ancient times, the Master usually required a disciple to maintain strict *secrecy* about his occult experiences. *Even a deep experience is likely to become weak through the contradiction and scepticism of others, unless the aspirant has learned to follow his own inner experience irrespective of what others might think or say.* If the aspirant is to make quick progress and to profit most through occult help, he must develop immense and unshakable confidence in himself and the Master. He must not look to others for guidance, because *those who will understand his problems or his experiences are very few.* The aspirant must, indeed, be prepared to face the possibility of not being thoroughly understood by all his friends or relations, for they might be in the dark about the grounds for his ideology and course of action.

If at the time of its occurrence an occult experience has served the purpose of giving new momentum to

Effect of doubt on potency of occult experience

spiritual endeavour, it often does not matter if the aspirant considers it in retrospective analysis and thought as being a form of delusion. However, *there are some occult experiences which are deliberately vouchsafed to the aspirant in order that they should be a standing source of inspiration and guidance.* With regard to these special experiences, it becomes necessary that the aspirant should cease to doubt their validity and importance. But the general attitude to seek endless corroborations of occult experiences is definitely unhealthy, and the Master gives corroborative confirmation only when he considers it necessary. Further, he takes the initiative in the way he judges best in the situation. Whatever he does arises from his *unfettered discretion* and is in no way related to or dependent upon any expectation developed by the aspirant. But when it is spiritually necessary the Master does increase the efficacy of occult experience *by confirming its validity and authority through some direct or indirect corroboration* from the aspirant's normal range of experience.

In the advancing stages to the beginning of the Path, the aspirant becomes spiritually prepared for being entrusted with free use of the forces of the inner

Astral journeys world of the astral bodies. He may then get used to undertaking astral journeys in his astral body, after leaving the physical body in sleep or wakefulness. The astral journeys which are undertaken unconsciously are much less important than those undertaken with full consciousness and as a result of deliberate volition. This implies conscious use of the astral body. Conscious separation of the astral body from the outer vehicle of the gross body has its own value in making the soul feel its distinction from the gross body and in arriving at a fuller control of the gross body. One can, at will, put on and put off the external gross body, as if it were a cloak, and use the astral body for experiencing the inner world of the astral and undertaking journeys through it, if and when necessary.

The sights, smells, tastes, contacts and sounds which are experienced through conscious use of the astral body are clear and definite, like the experiences

Enlarged scope for advancement

gained through conscious use of the gross body. They are not vague or subjective, as in ordinary dreams, but are as objective and effective as other experiences of wakeful consciousness. The ability to undertake astral journeys therefore involves considerable expansion of one's scope for experience. It brings opportunities for promoting one's own spiritual advancement, which begins with the involution of consciousness.

The harnessing of occult forces is not to be regarded in any way as a substitute for the inner effort which the aspirant must make to advance further.

Occult experience an aid to intuition, not its substitute

When occult experiences are gifts from the Masters or spiritually advanced souls, they serve the purpose of unveiling much of the hitherto obscured intuition, removing some of the difficulties on the Path and filling the aspirant with the great confidence and enthusiasm which are necessary to cope with the new requirements of each stage of the Path. But the aspirant makes real progress by putting into practice the best intuitions of his heart, not by being the merely passive recipient of occult experiences.

The Place of Occultism in Spiritual Life

PART II
THE OCCULT BASIS OF SPIRITUAL LIFE

THOSE who have even a preliminary acquaintance with the structure and laws of the inner spheres of existence know that complete isolation of human beings is a figment of imagination. Whether they desire it or not, all persons are constantly acting and interacting upon each other by their very existence, even when they do not establish any contact on the physical plane. There are no limits to the spreading of the influence of man. The magnetic influence of the subtle spheres knows no barriers of national frontiers or any other conventional limitations. Good thoughts as well as evil thoughts, cheerful moods as well as gloomy moods, noble and expansive feelings as well as petty and narrow emotions, unselfish aspiration as well as selfish ambition—all these have a tendency to spread out and influence others, even when they are not expressed in words or deeds. *The world of mental life is as much a unified system as the world of gross matter*. The gross world as a vehicle of spiritual life has its own indubitable importance, but the links and connections existing

People constantly interacting on inner planes

between different persons can by no means be fully estimated if we merely consider the tangible transactions which take place in the gross world.

For an aspirant to see saints and masters does not yield its full significance except in the context of all the corresponding happiness of the inner planes. The ancient *Rishis* have attached

Value of *darshana* and *sahavasa*

great importance to having the *darshana* of saints and masters, because *they are the source of the constant flow of love and light which emanates from them and makes an irresistible appeal to the inner feeling of the aspirant even when he receives no verbal instruction from them.* The effect of *darshana* is dependent upon the receptivity and response of the aspirant, whose reaction is determined by his own *sanskaras* and past connections. Often the aspirant is completely satisfied with the *darshana* of the Master and he desires nothing further from him. To derive bliss and contentment from the mere *darshana* of the Master is a great thing because it indicates that the aspirant has desirelessness and love, which are the two essentials of spiritual life. Having had the *darshana* of the supreme Beloved, the aspirant naturally desires nothing except to have more of his *darshana*, and is thus impelled by his inner spiritual urge to seek the *sahavasa* (company) of the Master as often as possible. Further *sahavasa* of the Master implements and strengthens the purifying effect of *darshana* and also results in drawing the aspirant closer and closer to the Master on the inner planes of life.

Like *darshana*, falling at the feet of the Master also has a special value of its own. The feet, which are physically the lowest part of the body, are the highest from the spiritual point of view. Physically the feet

Feet of the Master go through everything—good and bad, beautiful and ugly, clean and dirty, yet they remain above everything. Spiritually the feet of the Master are above everything in the universe, which is like dust to them. *When people come to a Perfect Master and touch his feet with their hands, they lay the burden of their sanskaras on him.* He collects the *sanskaras* from all over the universe, just as an ordinary person, in walking, collects dust on his feet. There is a hoary custom that after the aspirant has the *darshana* of the Master and falls at his feet, he washes the Master's feet with milk and honey and places a coconut near them as his offering. Honey represents red *sanskaras*, milk represents white *sanskaras* and the coconut represents the mind. Thus this convention which has become established in some areas in connection with greeting the Masters, really symbolises throwing the burden of all *sanskaras* on the Master and surrendering the mind to him. Adoption of this inner attitude constitutes the most critical and important step which the aspirant must take in order to get initiated on the Path.

Once the aspirant has the bliss of the *darshana* of a Master, that sight gets carved on his mind, and even when he is unable to establish frequent personal contact,

Mental contact his mind turns to the Master again and again in an effort to understand His significance. This process of establishing mental contact with the Master is essentially different from merely imaginative revival of past incidents. In the ordinary play of imagination, the recall of past incidents is not necessarily animated by a definite purpose, whereas in establishing mental contact there is a definite purpose. Owing to the *directive power of purpose*, imagination ceases to be a mere revolving of ideas and reaches out to the Master through the inner planes and establishes contact with him. Such mental contact with the Master is often as fruitful and effective as his physical *darshana*. The inward repetition of such mental contacts is like constructing a channel between Master and aspirant, who becomes thereby the recipient of the grace, love and light which are constantly flowing from the Master in spite of the apparent distance between them. Thus, *the help of the Master goes out not only to those who happen to be in his physical presence but also to others who establish mental contact with him.*

The Master devotes careful attention to the individual needs of the disciple and the first thing he does is to protect the disciple from influences that

Special precautions indicated by certain occult conditions

will divert his attention from the Path or interfere with his progress. Often the Master requires the disciple to accept some kind of temporary isolation so that his mind is guarded against impacts which might impede his spiritual progress. The ancient *yogis*, under instructions from their Masters, prepared their own food and did not allow anyone to remain present at the time of eating it. The reason was to avoid impressions of evil from the glance of bad persons. A disciple is also likely to catch the impressions of another's lust just as a clean cloth may be readily soiled by dirt. In the earlier stages the aspirant must guard against any complications which might arise through association with others who are not on the Path. But *the Master gives special instructions for the severance or avoidance of certain connections and contacts only when they are specially indicated for the special case*. In most cases, however, all that is necessary is secured merely by the constant company of the Master, and no need arises to submit the disciple to actual isolation. Although the disciple may be outwardly in touch with the world, he remains mentally detached from it because of his inward connection with the Master.

Just as the Master may isolate a close disciple from undesirable contacts and connections, he may also actually encourage and bring about new and fresh

Helpful contacts and associations

contacts which he deems to be in the spiritual interest of the disciple. He has a consummate understanding of the *sanskaras* and *karmic* ties and their complications, and he can consciously help people to enter into such associations as will allow and call forth important responses and activities, and help the progress of all concerned along the line of least resistance or by the shortest possible route. *He uses his knowledge of the past lives, sanskaras and connections of people to help them economise their spiritual energy and use it with best results.*

The unity and solidarity of the inner plane makes it possible for the Master to use his disciple as a medium for his work even when the disciple is unconscious of

The disciple as a medium

serving this larger purpose of the Master. This is possible because the disciple, through his love and understanding of the Master as well as his obedience and surrender, establishes a rapport with the Master and comes into tune with him. Those who come into direct contact with the Master receive his direct help, and those who are closely connected with his disciple receive the Master's indirect help.

Sharing of spiritual work is by no means one-sided; even the disciples who merely think of the Master or meditate upon him have the privilege of sharing the spiritual and universal work in which the Master might

The Master as a relaying station

be engaged at that moment. As he is one with eternity, the Master is beyond time and all limitations of time; as he is also interested in the spiritual upliftment of humanity, he assumes many of the limitations of time and his work can be helped by the voluntary co-operation of his disciples. *The Master feeds upon the love of his disciples and utilises the spiritual forces released by them for his universal work.* In this way the Master is like the *relaying station* which receives a song only in order to broadcast it to the world at large. To love the Master is to love all, not merely symbolically but actually; for what the Master receives on the subtle planes he spiritualises and distributes. Thus he not only strengthens the personal links which the disciples may have with him but also gives them the privilege of sharing his divine work.

By infinite ways, the Master tries to draw the aspirant into his own being so that he may get disentangled from the mazes of the universe and come to

The internal eye

desire God. This longing for God is present in the aspirant from the very beginning, but the Master makes this primary longing more intense and articulate by opening the internal eye of the aspirant. *When the internal eye is opened God, who is the object of search and longing, is actually sighted.* As the gaze of the soul is turned inward and fixed upon the supreme reality, the desire to establish union with it becomes much more ardent than when the soul is groping for God through mere speculation or imagination. When the time is ripe the Master can open this internal eye in less than a second.

Ultimately the aspirant has to realise that God is the only Reality and that he is really one with God.

This implies that he should not be overpowered
Om-point by the spectacle of the multi-
form universe. In fact, *the
whole universe is in the Self and springs into existence from
the tiny point in the Self which is referred to as "Om"*. But
the self has become habituated to gathering experience
through one medium or another, and therefore it comes
to experience the universe as a formidable rival other
than itself. Those who have realized God constantly
see the universe as springing from this "*Om*-point"
which is in everyone.

The process of perception runs parallel to the
process of creation, and the reversing of the process of
perception without obliterating consciousness amounts
Reversing process to realising the nothingness
of perception of the universe as a separate
entity. The Self sees first
through the mind, then through the subtle eye and
lastly through the physical eye; and it is *vaster than
all that it can perceive*. The big ocean and the vast spaces
of the sky are tiny as compared with the Self. In fact,
*all that the Self can perceive is finite, but the Self itself is
infinite*. When the Self retains full consciousness and
yet sees nothing, it has crossed the universe of its own
creation and has taken the first step to know itself as
everything.

The entire process of withdrawing consciousness
from the universe and becoming conscious of the Self
is accompanied by an increasing control of all the
Siddhis vehicles of consciousness. Such
control is made possible by
the vivification and activation of unused *centres of
control;* and the functioning of new centres brings in its
train a number of occult powers. These new powers
are commonly known as *siddhis*, and they can come be-

fore the aspirant has become spiritually perfect. In fact, egoism can flourish through the acquisition of such occult powers. The aspirant may not only take delight in possessing them, but might actually use them for mundane purposes from which he has not necessarily freed himself. *Siddhis* are therefore rightly regarded as obstacles to the attainment of realisation. However, after God is realised all these occult powers dwindle in their importance. *The siddhis have their field in the nothingness which is the universe, and the person who realises God is permanently and immovably established in the Supreme Reality.* Although the whole universe is like a zero to the God-realised person, he may voluntarily assume responsibility toward those souls who are enmeshed in the tangles of the universe. In that case he can freely and legitimately make use of his occult powers for the spiritual good of others.

There is nothing which does not admit of direct or indirect control by the Masters of wisdom. Large social phenomena such as wars, revolutions and epidemics, as **Furtherance of the divine plan** well as cosmic phenomena such as earthquakes, floods and other changes, are equally amenable to their control and direction through the release of the forces of the exalted planes on which the Masters are consciously stationed. The Masters can also use the occult forces and possibilities for securing *co-operative and co-ordinated spiritual work*. They frequently hold meetings and conferences on the higher planes for securing the advancement of humanity. *The Over-soul in all is only One and It always functions as a unity.* Those who have become conscious of this unity become fit to undertake unlimited responsibility, because they have shed the lower limitations of the human mind and have become so impersonal and universal in their interest that *they are effective vehicles for the execution and furtherance of the Divine Plan on earth.*

The Place of Occultism in Spiritual Life

PART III
OCCULTISM AND SPIRITUALITY

OCCULTISM is a branch of knowledge concerned with the study of the universe and human personality. In this respect there is no difference of principle

Occultism as a science

between occultism and other sciences concerned with the study of these subjects. The difference between occultism and other sciences arises because other sciences are concerned with aspects and forces directly or indirectly accessible to ordinary observation and manipulation, whereas *occultism is concerned with those hidden aspects and forces which are essentially inaccessible to ordinary observation and manipulation.* The development of occult knowledge is conditioned by the unfoldment of the latent powers of the human spirit.

Many of the psychical research societies of modern times approach occult knowledge with the same attitude which characterises other forms of knowledge,

Limitations on spread of occultism as a science

because in principle there seems to be no reason why it should be regarded as either less valuable or more valuable than other forms of theoretical knowledge. We find these societies trying to pursue occult knowledge in an organised and co-operative form. The Masters have also deemed it desirable at times to reveal to the generality of mankind some theoretical knowledge about certain important features of the occult world such as immortality and reincarnation, the existence of different bodies and planes and the laws concerning evolution and the operation of *Karma*. Such knowledge gives the right sort of background for spiritual aspiration and effort, and brings the perspective of the average man as near to the truth as is possible under the circumstances. *With the exception of such general knowledge about fundamentals, however, the Masters have consistently preferred to attach minimum importance to the spread of detailed knowledge about occult realities, and have even scrupulously withheld information concerning those points likely to have vital bearing upon occultism as an art.*

In occultism, more than in any other science, there is a sharp and significant division between *those who know* and *those who do not know*. In other sciences, to a certain

Those who know and those who do not know

extent indirect knowledge can take the place of direct knowledge. In occultism, indirect knowledge can in no way approximate direct knowledge in import and significance. Therefore, though occultism is an important science, the spread of purely theoretical information about occult realities can have little importance. For those who have no first-hand experience of occult realities, purely theoretical acquaintance with some occult facts can have no special value. These occult realities are bound to remain for them more or less in the same category as descriptions of unseen lands or works of imagination.

Occultism as a science may be said to be more or less on

the same footing as other sciences, but occultism as an art stands by itself. However, even the spread of purely

Occultism as an art

theoretical information about occult facts is accompanied at times with mischief, since it is likely to arouse idle curiosity and stimulate craving for acquiring control over unknown forces with a view to using them for selfish ends. There is nothing particularly spiritual about occult power as such. Like any other mundane power or scientific invention, it is capable of being used for good ends or bad. It gives immense scope for co-operative work on the higher planes, but this necessarily implies a spiritual preparedness to shoulder a special responsibility.

The novice may seek some occult powers and, within certain limits, even succeed in having them, but this new attainment will prove to be a curse rather

Misuse of occult power

than a blessing if he is not spiritually prepared for the adequate fulfillment of the new responsibility implied in the acquisition of the new powers. Even the slightest misuse of occult power has a severe reaction and creates a binding for the soul. Sometimes it may retard the progress of the aspirant and may even lead to a considerable set-back. *Apart from the spiritual ruin which the novice may invite upon himself through indiscreet use of occult power, he is bound to be a source of incalculable harm to others over whom he has succeeded in wielding a formidable advantage.*

In the hands of the Masters of spiritual wisdom, occult power is not only safe but has immense capacity that can be harnessed in the service of humanity, but even they are very sparing and economical in its use. By its very nature, occultism as an art has its own natural limitations. It cannot be widely used for helping the

Occultism as an art to be restricted to furtherance of spiritual purposes

material needs of humanity or helping it in its mundane purposes. *The introduction of an uncertain and incalculable factor, which the free exercise of occult power would involve, is bound to create much confusion and disturbance in the ordinary pursuits of men, who must be left to their own limitations, resources and possibilities for the equal and uninterrupted working out of the law of Karma.* The use of occult power, therefore, has to be strictly restricted to the furtherance of *spiritual* purposes.

Sometimes the saints do fulfill some of the mundane desires of their devotees, but this is not done because they are interested in mundane affairs, but because

Material bait for spiritual interest

they are interested in weaning their devotees away from their material cravings. When children are very young they cannot be induced to attend to letters written on a slate. In order to induce their attention to letters the elders present them sometimes with letters specially constructed out of sweets. Then they attend to these letters, not because they are interrested in the letters as such, but because they are interested in the sweets. But this often proves to be the beginning of their interest in the letters themselves, and the sweets can soon be discarded after they have cultivated this interest. Worldly people are like such young children. Just as the father may occasionally give a piece of chocolate to the baby in order to encourage it to be good, the saints might give to their worldly minded devotees certain harmless objects they desire so that they may eventually be willing to part with them and get interested in true spirituality.

Worldly people are so much immersed in material cravings that nothing interests them unless it has some direct bearing upon the fulfillment of these cravings.

Saints not to be approached with material motives

Yet they may come to saints and serve or respect them in the expectation of being helped in their material problems. *When a person approaches a saint with respect, it becomes the duty of the saint to help him spiritually even when he has come with some other motive.* The saint, with his larger understanding of the human mind, may therefore decide to help the person materially in order to win him over to true spirituality. Such offering of a material bait for spiritual purposes is an *exception* rather than a rule. Mostly the saints discourage people from approaching them for any material advantage. From the spiritual point of view it is infinitely better for a person to love saints simply because they are lovable, than to love them for some selfish ends. *People should go to saints because they are genuinely interested in true spirituality and for no other reason.* It is only then that they derive the greatest benefit from their contact with the saints.

Occultism as an art derives its justification solely from its capacity to subserve spiritual purposes; any diversion of occult power from this end may be looked

Occult powers used to promote purification of humanity

upon as misuse. It must not be summoned merely for worldly purposes. Its true function is not to secure the fulfillment of human cravings, but to secure the purification of the human heart. *Occultism as an art is among the most effective and potent factors which can contribute to the purging of humanity by helping it to give up baser desires.*

Occultism as an art becomes particularly relevant and necessary in the cases of those who, because of their evolution, are about to unfold their latent psychic powers, or those who already have considerably deve-

Special sphere for use of occult powers
loped psychic powers, but sometimes are not fully alive to the gross world owing to the withdrawal of their consciousness to the higher planes. They have to be spoken to *in a language which they can understand.* Many advanced aspirants develop a number of occult powers, but they are often as much in need of spiritual help as the ordinary run of humanity. As they are in possession of many occult powers they can be readily and effectively helped by Perfect Masters irrespective of distance. *When the Master's help can be consciously received on the higher planes, it becomes much more fruitful than the help which he can give merely through the gross medium.*

Apart from the difficulties existing in forward movement on the Path, one of the characteristics of advanced aspirants is to get so deeply established in the

Coming down
happiness of their station that they are reluctant to come down for work in the gross sphere. This coming down of advanced aspirants must not be confused with the return to normal consciousness after the 7th plane experience which is the state of God-realisation of Perfect Ones. *The Perfect Master's* return journey and consequent position in different planes after Realisation, is actuated by altruistic motives and is the result of *Prarabdha,* which the Perfect Ones utilise for the spiritual uplift of humanity in accordance with the authority with which they are vested. For instance, it is said Mohammed stationed himself after God-realisation in the 7th plane, Buddha in the 5th and Moenuddin Chisti of Ajmer in the 5th, though they are conscious of all the planes simultaneously.

The coming down of advanced *aspirants* is induced in order to help accelerate their forward movement on the Path when they find themselves hung up anywhere betwixt the planes. For example, when an aspirant gets hung up somewhere between the 3rd and 4th planes, a Master usually brings him down to the 3rd plane prior to pushing him up to the 4th plane. Such coming down from their high station is also often necessary in the interest of those who are still in the wilderness of the world and have not even entered the Path. *The Master may sometimes decide to get some spiritual work done through an advanced aspirant and may require him to postpone his efforts for individual advancement for the sake of others.* Such coming down eventually turns out to be a spiritual preparation for traversing the next stage of the Path smoothly and quickly; but even so, the aspirant finds it difficult to renounce the advantages of his attainment for the purpose of helping others. Coming down is particularly difficult for a person intensely experiencing a state of enchantment. In Sufism, this enchantment is known as *Hairat*. In this state the aspirant finds it extremely difficult to keep away from different kinds of enchantment. But sometimes, it is necessary that he should resist getting lost in enchantment and *come down for the sake of others in the world*. The Master has his own way of dealing with an advanced aspirant and he can bring him round to any unpalatable move.

This is very well illustrated in the story of a famous *Vali* named Ganjay Shakkar (Baba Fariduddin). Much before he could get illumination this *Vali* could not

Story of Ganjay Shakkar

close his eyes, which were always open, dazed and glassy; and he could not eat as he was in *Hairat* and completely enchanted in that state. His Master, the Khwaja of Ajmer, wanted him to keep away from this state of enchantment and come down, but he found it difficult to obey his Master. Then the Master turned the key and brought him round in the following manner. He inwardly inspired five thieves to come near the place of this *Vali*. They sat within five paces from this *Vali* and began to share the plunder which they had stolen. Soon they began quarrelling with each other and two of them killed the other three. These two, who were successful in the quarrel, divided the loot between them and ran away. But while running away they passed by the place where the *Vali* was sitting. As soon as they came near the *Vali* he regained normal consciousness. The proximity of these criminals was sufficient crude stimulus to bring him down to consciousness. The first thing that he saw was some sparrows and his first impulse was to try his nascent powers on them. He said, "O sparrows, die," and the sparrows fell down dead. Then he said, "Sparrows, rise up," and they rose. The two thieves who saw this were amazed and they requested the *Vali* to raise the three thieves whom they had killed in a moment of anger. On this the *Vali* addressed himself to the three dead thieves and said, "Rise up," but they did *not* rise. He was aghast at the thought that he had lost his powers, and repenting for the frivolous use of his powers, he went crying to his Master. When he came near the Master he saw that those three thieves were massaging the feet of his Master. The *Vali* then went back to his original place, indifferent to food or drink. He became lean and remained stationed in the same spot for ten years until white ants began to eat up his body. People used to come to the *Vali* and place near his body large quantities of sugar which the ants ate. Since his body was always surrounded by heaps of sugar he came to be known as *Ganjay Shakkar*, or the treasury of sugar. His story shows how even the most advanced aspirants need the help of the Master if they are to proceed further on the way to realisation.

Ganjay Shakkar's story illustrates the sort of occasion which calls forth the use of occult methods and occult powers, but it must be carefully noted that

Occult phenomena have no intrinsic value

no occult phenomenon, regardless of grade, can have any intrinsic value in itself. *The value which seems to belong to phenomena—occult or non-occult—is either purely illusory or entirely relative.* Illusory values arise when anything acquires false importance, because it stimulates or promises to fulfill the passing cravings and the limited purposes born of ignorance. If the thing is taken out of the context of these passing cravings and limited purposes, it is immediately deprived of the entire meaning with which it seemed to be surcharged. Relative values arise when a thing acquires importance through serving the realisation or expression of the Truth. The importance of such things is derived from their being the essential conditions for the game of divine life; and therefore, though it is relative, such value is real and not illusory.

Most persons consciously or unconsciously attach undue importance to occult phenomena and mistake them for spirituality. For them, miracles and spirit-

Occultism to be distinguished from spirituality

phenomena are the real topics of absorbing interest, and this is presumed to indicate an interest in the true life of the spirit. *There is a very clear and definite distinction, however, between occultism and mysticism, spiritualism and spirituality*; and any failure to grasp the full import of this difference can only lead to confusion.

All miracles belong to the phenomenal world,

which is the world of shadows. As phenomena, they are subject to change, and nothing that changes can have

The only thing that matters

lasting value. Realisation of the eternal Truth is an initiation into the unchangeable Being, which is the supreme Reality; and *no acquaintance with the occult world or capacity to manipulate its forces can really amount to realisation of the Truth.* Occult phenomena are as much within the domain of false imagination as are ordinary phenomena of the gross world. From the spiritual point of view the only important thing is to realise the Divine Life and help others to realise it by manifesting it in every-day happenings. *To penetrate into the essence of all being and significance and to release the fragrance of that inner attainment for the guidance and benefit of others, by expressing, in the world of forms, truth, love, purity and beauty—this is the sole game which has intrinsic and absolute worth. All other happenings, incidents and attainments in themselves can have no lasting importance.*

The Types of Meditation

PART I

THE NATURE OF MEDITATION
AND ITS CONDITIONS

MEDITATION may be described as *the path which the individual cuts for himself while trying to get beyond the limitations of the mind*. If a man caught up in the tangles of a thick forest tries to get out into the open, his efforts to break through the encircling impediments will leave behind him the marks of his journey. By the study of these marks an observer will be able to describe the paths which he traversed in his attempt to come out into the open. The movements of the man who comes out of the forest are different in principle from those of the railway engine which moves along rails already laid on the course it is to take. The man is not following a ready-made path; *the path becomes imprinted after he has traversed it*. In the same way, the man who finds himself drawn into deep meditation is really grappling with the spiritual problems that he faces. He is not merely trying to adhere to a rigid line of movement that already exists in his mental make-up.

Meditation is the path forged by the individual while controlling mind

The development of meditation can nevertheless be *anticipated* in outline by those who have direct insight into the peculiar contours of the mind of the individual,

General lines of meditation can be anticipated

in the same way that a person who has thorough acquaintance with the details of the constitution of the solidified crust of the earth may, in general, expect the outburst of a volcano in one region rather than another. When the surging powers in the bowels of the earth are trying to burst out, they are bound to take the line of least resistance, and their actual passage will be dependent largely upon the nature of the surroundings with which they are confronted. The difference between volcanic forces and the spiritual urge is that the former are unconscious, while the latter is a conscious phenomenon. Intelligence plays an important part in the course of meditation, and *it is this intelligence which is kindled by the Master by giving to the aspirant a few simple suggestions about what kinds of things he has to do or expect in his meditations.*

Meditation has often been misunderstood as a mechanical process of *forcing* the mind upon some idea or object. Most people naturally have an aversion to

Intelligent meditation sustained by interest

meditation because they experience great difficulty in attempting to coerce the mind in a particular direction, or to pin it down to one particular thing. *Any purely mechanical handling of the mind is not only irksome but is bound ultimately to be unsuccessful.*

The first principle which aspirants have to remember is that the mind can be controlled and directed in meditation *only according to laws inherent in the make-up of the mind itself,* and not by means of the application of any mechanical or semi-mechanical force.

Many persons who do not technically "meditate" are oftentimes found to be deeply and intensely engrossed in systematic and clear thinking about some practical problem or theoretical subject. Their mental process is, in a sense, very much like meditation, inasmuch as the mind is engrossed in intense thinking about a particular subject-matter to the exclusion of all other irrelevant things. Meditation is often easy and spontaneous in such mental processes because the mind is dwelling upon an object in which it is interested and which it increasingly understands. The spiritual tragedy about ordinary trains of thoughts is that they are not directed towards things that really matter. On the other hand, the object of meditation has always to be carefully selected and must be *spiritually important;* it has to be some divine person or object, or some spiritually significant theme or truth. In order to attain success in meditation the mind must not only get interested in the divine subjects or truths, but must also begin by trying to *understand and appreciate them.* Such intelligent meditation is a natural process of the mind; and since it avoids the monotonous rigidity and regularity of mechanical meditation, it becomes not only *spontaneous and inspiring, but easy and successful.*

Meditation should be distinguished from concentration. Meditation is the first stage of a process which gradually develops into concentration. *In concentration the mind seeks to unite with its* **Meditation and concentration** *object by the process of fixing itself upon that object, whereas meditation consists in thorough thinking about a particular object to the exclusion of every other thing.* In concentration there is practically no movement of the mind, but in meditation the mind moves from one relevant idea to another. In concentration the mind merely dwells upon some *form* or a pithy and terse *formula*, without amplifying it through a succession of ideas. In meditation the mind tries to understand and assimilate the object by dwelling upon diverse attributes of the form or various implications of the formula. In concentration as well as in meditation, there is a peaceful intermingling of love and longing for the divine object or principle on which the mind dwells, and both these psychic activities are very different from the merely *mechanical* processes which have rigid regularity and unrelieved monotony.

Persons with no capacity for intense concentration have to begin with meditation, whereas for those who have the capacity for concentration, meditation is unnecessary. It is sufficient if they concentrate on the mere form of a God-man or Man-God or on some simple formula like, "*I am neither the gross body nor the subtle body[1] nor the mental body[2]; I am Atman (Soul).*"

Meditation is essentially an individual matter in the sense that it is not for self-display in society, but for one's own spiritual advancement. Utter isolation of the

Silence and seclusion helpful for meditation

individual from social surroundings is almost always conducive to unhampered prosecution of meditation. The ancient *yogis* took to mountains and caves in search of complete seclusion. Great quiet and undisturbed silence are essential for attaining success. However, it is not necessary for persons to go to mountains and caves in search of these conditions. Even in towns a little care and trouble can secure for the aspirant the quiet, silence and seclusion necessary to facilitate and promote progress in the different forms of meditation.

Darkness or closing one's eyes is not absolutely

---

1 The subtle body is the seat of desires and vital forces.
2 The mental body is the seat of the mind.

necessary for meditation. If the aspirant is face to face with the object of meditation he may have a successful

Value of darkness meditation even when his eyes are open. But in most cases, getting away from all gross sight and sound is conducive to intensive meditation. To secure complete external silence involves careful selection of the spot for meditation, but one has only to close one's eyes in order to protect the mind from the disturbance of sights. Sometimes, when there is light, closing the eyes is not sufficient to ward off all visual stimulation. Then it is advisable to start meditation in complete darkness. Darkness normally promotes progress in meditation.

With regard to posture, there are no fixed rules. Any posture which is comfortable and hygienically unobjectionable may be adopted, so long as it contrib-

Posture for meditation utes to the alertness of the mind and does not induce sleep. The posture should not involve any physical tension or pain, because it then deflects the attention to the body itself. The body should, therefore, be completely relaxed as when going to sleep, but the usual position which is taken in sleep should be avoided because of its tendency to induce sleep. When the body has assumed a convenient and suitable posture, it is helpful to think of the head as the centre of the body. When the head is regarded as the centre it is easier to forget the body and to fix one's attention on the object of meditation.

It is desirable that the aspirant should maintain the same posture for each meditation. The previous associations which the posture has with his medita-

Importance of fixing spot, posture and hour tions endow it with a special capacity to induce and facilitate similar meditations. When the body has assumed the chosen posture it is, as it were, constantly under the subconscious suggestion that it must not any more obtrude upon consciousness and that it has to serve the purpose of meditation. Choosing the same spot and a fixed hour also has a salutary effect. Hence the aspirant must be serious about resorting to an identical place, posture and hour. Choice of the spot also involves consideration of occult associations and possibilities of the spot. Special importance is attached to meditating in holy places where the Masters themselves have lived or meditated.

The place, posture and hour of meditation all have their relative importance, which varies according to the peculiarities and history of the individual. The Master, therefore, often gives different instructions to each disciple to suit his individual case. However, where meditation has become habitual through constant practice, adherence to a fixed place, posture or time can be dispensed with and the aspirant can carry on his meditation at any time under any conditions. Even when he is walking he may be inwardly absorbed in meditation.

Meditation should not be resorted to with a heavy heart, as if one were taking castor oil. One has to be serious about meditation, but not grave or melancholy.

Meditation should be a joyous enterprise

Humour and cheerfulness not only do not interfere with the progress of meditation but actually contribute to it. Meditation should not be turned into a distasteful and tiresome thing. *The aspirant should freely allow himself the natural joy which is attendant upon successful meditation without getting addicted to it.* Meditation should be something like a picnic on the higher planes. Like excursions into new and beautiful natural surroundings, meditation brings with it a *sense of enthusiasm, adventure, peace and exhilaration.* All thoughts of depression, fear or worry have to be cut out completely if there is to be a really successful meditation.

Though meditation is essentially an individual matter, collective meditation has its own advantages. If different aspirants who are in harmony with each other take to the same line of

Collective meditation meditation together, their thoughts have a tendency to augment and strengthen each other. This is particularly noticeable when disciples of the same Master are collectively engaged in meditating upon their Master. If a collective meditation of this type is to yield its full advantage, each aspirant who participates must be concerned with the course of his own meditation and not with what others of the group are doing. Though he starts his meditation in the company of others, he has to lose himself in the object of his meditation. He has to be entirely oblivious of the whole world, including his body, and he has to be exclusively cognisant of the object agreed upon before the beginning of the meditation. When intelligently handled, collective meditation can be of immense help to *beginners*, although advanced aspirants can carry on by themselves.

In ordinary thinking the uninterrupted flow of relevant trains of ideas is common, but when the mind sets itself to systematic meditation, there is inevitably

Arising of disturbing thoughts a *reactionary tendency for irrelevant and contrary thoughts to emerge and create disturbances.* This is *the law of the mind* and the aspirant should not be upset by the appearance in consciousness of many contrary and unwholesome thoughts which had hitherto never made their appearance. *Meditation involves bringing the subconscious contents of the mind to the forefront of* *consciousness.* Like the conjurer who summons into existence many strange and unexpected things, the process of meditation invites many absurd and unwanted thoughts. The aspirant must expect and be prepared for all these disturbing thoughts and should exercise inexhaustible *patience* with unshakable confidence that ultimately all these disturbances will be overcome.

The last but not least important condition for attaining success in meditation is adoption of the *right technique* for handling disturbing thoughts and mental

Technique of dealing with disturbing thoughts

influences. It is useless to waste psychic energy by trying *directly* to combat and repress disturbing thoughts. Any such attempt involves giving further attention to them and they feed upon the very attention given for the purpose of repressing them, thereby being further strengthened and confirmed in consciousness. It is best to ignore them and turn to the object of meditation as early as possible without attaching any undue importance to the disturbing factors. *By recognising the irrelevance and worthlessness of disturbing thoughts, and the relative value and importance of the object of meditation, it becomes possible to let the disturbing thoughts die through sheer neglect, thus making the mind permanently steady in the object of meditation.*

The Types of Meditation

PART II

THE CHIEF TYPES OF MEDITATION
AND THEIR RELATIVE VALUE

MEDITATION is of different types which can be conveniently distinguished from each other on the basis of *three* distinct principles. They can be clas-

Types of meditation classified by three principles

sified either on the basis of the *function* meditation performs in spiritual advancement, or *the part of personality that is predominantly brought into play during the process of meditation, or the items of experience it tries to understand*. Of these three principles, any one can be adopted for the classification of the different types of meditation. The last principle will be used later while giving a detailed account of the different forms of meditation, as it is most suitable for *enumerative purposes*. This part will make use of the first two principles, as they are helpful in different ways in explaining the relative value of the various forms of meditation.

With reference to the *first* principle, meditation has to serve the purpose of *associating* consciousness with the eternal Truth, and of dissociating consciousness from the false and unimportant things of the phenomenal

Associative meditation and dissociative meditation

world. There thus arise *two* types of meditation. *Associative meditation* predominantly involves the *synthetic* activity of the mind (*Anwaya*), *and dissociative meditation* predominantly involves the *analytic* activity of the mind (*Vyatireka*). Associative meditation may be illustrated by the formula, "I am Infinite," and dissociative meditation may be illustrated by the formula, "I am not my desires."

Through associative meditation the aspirant tries to unite with the spiritual ideal as mentally constructed by him. Through dissociative meditation the aspirant tries to separate himself from

Respective functions of associative and dissociative meditation

the conditions which come to him as anti-spiritual. Associative meditation is a process of *assimilation* of the essentials of spiritual life; dissociative meditation is a process of *elimination* of those factors which prevent the life of the spirit.

Associative meditation is concerned with objects which are, so to say, selected from the land of light, and dissociative meditation is concerned with objects

Dissociative meditation paves way for associative meditation

which are parts of the land of shadows. The world of illusions, like the world of shadows, has a bewildering charm of its own. If a person is to succeed in getting out of the world of illusions and arrive at the Truth, he must develop resistance to the enticement of the world of illusions by repeated recognition of its real worthlessness, just as a person must develop discontent with the world of shadows if he is to come into the light. Therefore dissociative meditation is a preliminary to associative meditation. It comes first and has its own value, but it is meant merely to pave the way for associative meditation.

Associative meditation and dissociative meditation are both necessary in a way, but eventually associative meditation turns out to be far more fruitful and important than dissociative meditation. If a person is surrounded by shadows, it does not help very much to be continuously upset about them. If he has no interest except that of being cross with the shadows, there will be no end to his worries. But if, instead of fretting and fuming about the engulfing shadows, he sets himself to the more important task of bringing himself under the full blaze of the sun, he will discover that all the shadows have disappeared. *What really matters is not aimless discontent with existing limitations but directive effort towards the established ideal.* As long as the person is turned towards the sun and he is trying to walk into the light, the shadows which encircle him cannot be a serious handicap to his emancipation. In the same way the aspirant need not worry too much about his failings, as long as his heart is firmly set upon uniting with his spiritual ideal. His failings will all have vanished into nothingness when his pilgrimage ends.

Associative meditation more fruitful than dissociative meditation

Associative meditation is to the spirit what the assimilation of food is to the body. The body can make up for its deficiencies by assimilating the right sort of food. Similarly the mind can secure its health by the assimilation of spiritual truths through meditation. It is necessary to strike a balance between the different forms of associative meditation even though in their own way they are all good, just as it is necessary to attend to balancing the diet even when one has satisfied oneself

Analogy of food

as to the nutritive value of the different components of the diet. Disproportionate development of mental life hampers advancement because of the internal fracturing which accompanies it, and *happy combinations of the different forms of meditation facilitate rapid progress because they secure a harmonised and balanced mind.* The right combinations are those which promote an *advancing equilibrium* by emphasising just those aspects of the truth which are relevant to removing the special obstacles, with which the aspirant is faced at the moment.

The analogy of diet can be extended even to the second type of meditation, which consists in avoiding and eliminating things which are anti-spiritual. As

Extension of the analogy

faulty diet can upset physical health, so faulty types of meditation can throw the mind into disorder. As the wrong type of food can ruin health instead of nourishing it, so instinctive meditation on the objects of craving creates further fetters for the mind instead of breaking those which already exist. *Therefore it is as important to avoid the wrong type of meditation as it is to avoid the wrong type of food.* Further, just as good health requires constant elimination of waste products and poisonous substances, spiritual health requires the *expulsion of undesirable thoughts and emotions.*

So far our explanations have differentiated the two types of meditation which may be observed from the standpoint of the *function* which meditation per-

Second principle covers three types of meditation

forms in spiritual advancement. It is equally illuminating to understand the different types of meditation into which the process of meditation is differentiated by considering the nature of the *part of the personality which is predominantly brought into play during the process of meditation.*

Through the application of this *second* principle we have *three* distinct types of meditation.

In the first type of meditation the intellect is predominantly brought into play; it might be called "*discriminative meditation*." In the second type the heart is predominantly brought into play; it might be called the "*meditation of the heart*." In the third type the active nature of man is predominantly brought into play; it might be called "*the meditation of action*."

Discriminative meditation, meditation of the heart and meditation of action

Discriminative meditation is represented by intellectual assertion of a formula like "I am not my body, but the Infinite." The meditation of the heart is represented by a steady and unhampered flow of love from the aspirant to the Divine Beloved. The meditation of action is represented by an unreserved dedication of one's life to the selfless service of the Master or humanity. Of these three types, meditation of the heart is the highest and most important, but the other two types also have their own value and cannot be neglected without serious detriment to the spiritual progress of the aspirant.

The different types of meditation must not be looked upon as being entirely exclusive of each other. They can proceed in all sorts of combinations. Some-

Different types of meditation usually supplement each other

times one type of meditation inevitably leads to another type, and progress in one type of meditation is often held up until there is corresponding progress in the other types. All the different types of meditation are valuable for securing the spiritual advancement of the aspirant. They almost always make up for mutual deficiencies and supplement each other.

One type of meditation may also interfere seriously

with the progress of another type if it is resorted to at an inopportune moment. The different types of genuine

One type of meditation may interfere with another

meditation all dwell upon aspects of life which are equally true; but *depending upon the psychic state of the individual, the assimilation of a certain truth of life is often more urgently necessary than the assimilation of some other truths of life.* Therefore the Masters never prescribe the same form of meditation to all, but give specific instructions according to the *individual needs of the aspirant.*

The type of meditation necessary in a particular situation often cannot be correctly ascertained by the aspirant for himself. *The aspirant can get addicted to one*

Need for specific instructions from the Master

type of meditation so exclusively that he finds it difficult to get out of the groove which has been cut into his mind by the type of meditation he has been practising. He fails to see the importance of any other type of meditation and is not drawn by it. Of course the aspirant himself may come to feel his own deficiency along a particular line, but just as many medicines are disagreeable to the patient, so the types of meditation that are really indicated in a specific situation often seem distasteful to the aspirant, and he is disinclined to take to them. The help and advice of the Master are indispensable on this point. The insight which the Master has into the deeper and real spiritual needs of the aspirant is infinitely greater than the insight which the aspirant can hope to have into himself. *Specific instructions from the Master supply the necessary corrective for the neglected aspects of personality.*

Although the aspirant may start with an initial aversion to the type of meditation he needs, he becomes interested in it when he sees its real value and purpose.

**True value of medita-
tion perceived only
in its practice**
He can come to appreciate the real value and purpose of a particular type of meditation only when he has tried it. It is not possible to discover the value and possibilities of any type of meditation by purely theoretical speculation about that mode of meditation. Such purely theoretical guesswork may have some superficial results but it fails to fathom the real utility of meditation. *Like many other things of spiritual importance, meditation yields its full significance after the person has gotten into it and not when he is trying to understand it by envisaging it from outside.*

In order to have real success in any mode of meditation, the aspirant must launch upon it with the determination to explore all its possiblities. He must not

**Determination neces-
sary for success in
meditation**
start with any limiting reservations, but should be prepared to encounter unexpected states of consciousness; and he should be willing to go where that line of meditation leads him without making any rigid demands based on preformed expectations. *The very essence of meditation is one-pointedness and the exclusion of all other considerations, even when these considerations happen to be enticing.*

However, if the aspirant takes to any type of meditation on his own initiative and without having the benefit of the guidance and supervision of the

**Supervision of Master
is indispensable**
Master, *he may get into it so far that he loses his perspective and is unable to recover himself.* It may be impossible for him to change over to some other complementary mode of meditation, even when it is absolutely necessary. This risk is avoided if the aspirant has taken to a line of meditation on the orders of his Master. When he is under the guidance and supervision

of the Master, the Master not only can ask the aspirant to halt at the right time, but he can actually help him also to get out of the grooves cut by his previous meditation.

In this connection there is an illustrative story of a man who was highly intelligent and who wanted to know from personal experience what it feels like for a

An illustrative story

man to be suffocated by being hung. He was not content merely with imagining what it would be like, but wanted to experience it himself. So he asked a friend to help him perform the experiment. He said that he would be hanged by a rope and would signal to his friend when the feeling of suffocation reached the danger limit. He further asked his friend not to relieve him from the gallows before he received the intended signal. His friend agreed to all this, and the man was hung by tying a rope round his own neck. But when he got suffocated he became unconscious, and therefore he could not give his friend the promised signal. The friend, however, was wise, and finding that the suffocation of the man had really reached the dangerous point, he went beyond the limits of his agreement and relieved the man just in time to save his life. The man could be saved not through his own thoughtfulness and precautions, but through the wise discretion of his friend. In the same way, *it is safer for the aspirant to rely upon the Master than upon any provisions of his own making.*

The Types of Meditation

PART III

GENERAL CLASSIFICATION OF THE FORMS OF MEDITATION

THE process of meditation aims at *understanding and transcending the wide and varied range of experience.* When meditation is interpreted in this manner, it is at

Meditation an attempt to understand experience

once seen to be something which is not peculiar to a few aspirants. It turns out to be a *process in which every living creature is engaged in some way.*

The tiger intent upon devouring a lamb that it has spied, "meditates" upon the lamb. The lamb in its turn having sighted the tiger, "meditates" upon the tiger.

Meditation is universal

The man who waits on the platform for the train is "meditating" upon the train, and the driver of the train, who expects to be relieved at the next station, is "meditating" upon the station. The scientist who works upon an unsolved problem "meditates" upon that problem. The patient who is waiting with tense anxiety for a doctor is "meditating" upon the doctor; and the doctor who is awaiting payment of his bill is "meditating" upon the account. When the policeman tries to catch a thief, they both "meditate" upon each other. The person who "falls in love" is "meditating" upon the beloved; the man who is jealously watchful of his rival is "meditating" upon his rival; the man struck with grief at the bereavement of a friend is "meditating" upon the friend; and the person who seeks revenge upon his enemy "meditates" upon his enemy. The man lost in making himself presentable by suitable clothing is "meditating" upon himself as the body; and the person who boasts of his intellectual or psychic attainments is "meditating" upon himself as the mind.

All these are, in a way, forms of "meditation," but in spiritual discourses the term meditation is usually restricted to those forms of meditation which tackle the

Spiritually important meditation is conscious of its aim

problem of understanding experience *intensively* and *systematically*. In the above examples, meditation is a result of natural application of the mind to the objects with which it is presented. In this application of the mind the subject is almost unconscious of the ultimate purpose of the process of meditation. In the spiritual field, however, meditation in the initial stages at least is deliberate. During such meditation the subject is more specifically conscious of the ultimate objective. Nevertheless, the forms of meditation characteristic of the spiritual field are *continuous* with those found throughout the world of consciousness, *the spiritual forms of meditation springing into existence only when the other more general forms of meditation have brought the person to a certain crisis or "blind alley."* Then he is forced to choose his object of meditation in the light of some spiritual ideal and must also revise the manner of meditation to which he may have become accustomed.

The spiritually important forms of meditation are of two kinds: (1) *General* meditation, which consists in the assimilation of the Divine Truths, and (2) *Specialised*

General meditation and specialised meditation

meditation, in which the mind *selects* some definite item of experience and is *exclusively* concerned with it. General meditation is only a carrying further of the ordinary thought-processes systematically and intensively. It is different from the many pre-spiritual meditations of the *non-sadhaka* (worldly) only in so far as (i) the thought processes now come to be directed towards realities which have spiritual importance, and (ii) the mind makes intelligent use of the expositions of the Divine Truths given by those who *know*, without renouncing its critical powers and inherent zest for the Truth.

The specialised forms of meditation, on the other hand, imply and require something more than a purely intellectual approach to the Truth. In the specialised

Specialised meditation aims at more than intellectual understanding

forms of meditation, as in general meditation, the mind has an opportunity to have an *intellectual* understanding of the object of meditation, but in addition they also help *to cultivate mental discipline, develop capacities hitherto dormant, and unfold latent possibilities of personality.*

The problem in specialised forms of meditation is not theoretical but practical. *Specialised forms of meditation are helpful for overcoming specific obstacles in the way of*

Problem for specialised meditation is practical

enlightenment and realisation; they aim at controlling the mind and going beyond it. Specialised forms of meditation are more like the desperate attempts of a man to break through the walls of his prison, than like the idle speculative activity that is involved in forming "opinions" about the strength of the different parts of the prison-walls, or about what may be visible after breaking into the open.

In spiritual life, even a sincere mistake taken seriously may have more value than half-hearted allegiance to theoretical or formal truth. The *practical* purpose in the specialised

Practical purpose may over-ride formal truth

forms of meditation must sometimes prevail *even at the cost of formal and theoretical truth.* Thus, while concentrating on a particular formula or form, no other formula or form can be allowed access to the mind although, intrinsically, this other formula or form may have the same or even greater spiritual importance. If an aspirant has been meditating upon one Master, he has to exclude from his mind all ideas of any other Masters, though these Masters may be as perfect as the Master on whom he is meditating. In the same way, intensive thinking might be as helpful in achieving the goal as the process of making the mind blank.

As a rule, *mixing* up of the specialised forms of meditation is not desirable, though theoretically they may equally be directed towards different aspects of the

Function of general meditation

Truth. *The task of bringing together the different facets of the Truth and building up a whole and complete view of life is attempted by general meditation,* in which thought is free, comprehensive and receptive to all aspects of the Truth. Such general meditation has its own value and justification. *General meditation is helpful before specialised forms of meditation as well as after trying them,* but it cannot take the place of specialised forms of meditation because these have a different purpose and function.

The different forms of specialised meditation are comparable to different forms of bodily *exercise*, which may have some specific purpose. Exercise of the muscles

Specialised meditation like specific exercise

is meant only to strengthen the muscles, but this does not mean that the muscles are the only important part of the body. All types of exercise are important for securing the general health of the body, although it may not be possible to take all of them at the same time.

The functions of the different specialised forms of exercise have, however, to be correlated and governed in the light of our knowledge of true health or propor-

General meditation and specialised meditation not interchangeable

tionate development of the body. In the same way, the functions of the specialised forms of meditation have to be correlated with and gov-

erned by the whole and complete ideal of life. This the aspirant constructs through the process of *general* meditation or *unrestrained thought, which knows no law except that of finding the Truth in all its aspects. Just as specialised forms of meditation cannot be replaced by general meditation, so general meditation also cannot be replaced by specialised forms of meditation*. Both are necessary and have their own value.

For enumerative purposes, the different specialised forms of meditation can be conveniently classified *on the basis of those items of experience which the mind tries to under-*

Different specialised meditations

stand. Human experience, in all its variety, is throughout characterised by the dual

aspect of subject and object. Some forms of meditation are concerned with the *objects of experience;* some are

concerned with the *subject of experience;* and some forms
of meditation are concerned with the *mental operations*
which are involved in the interaction of the subject and
the object. Thus we define *three* kinds of meditation.

All the forms of meditation which the aspirant
(*sadhak*) might adopt ultimately culminate in the goal
of all meditation, which is to get established in *Sahaj*

Table of General Classification of the Types
of Meditation

A	THE VARIED FORMS OF MEDITATION BEFORE A PERSON BECOMES AN ASPIRANT (*Sadhaka*)				
B	FORMS OF THE MEDITATION OF THE ASPIRANT	i	General Meditation or the assimilation of the Divine Truth	1	Philosophical thinking
				2	Hearing a discourse from the Masters
				3	Reading the written expositions of the Masters
		ii	Specialised Meditation which selects some definite items of experience	1	Meditation concerned with the *objects* of experience
				2	Meditation concerned with the *subject* of experience
				3	Meditation concerned with *mental operations*
C	*SAHAJ SAMADHI* OR THE MEDITATION OF THOSE WHO ARE SPIRITUALLY PERFECT (*Siddha*)			1	*Nirvana* or Absorption
				2	*Nirvikalpa State* or Divinity in Expression

Two forms of *Sahaj Samadhi*

Samadhi or spontaneous meditation of the spiritually perfected soul. *Sahaj Samadhi* has two forms: (i) *Nirvana or Absorption* and (ii) *Nirvikalpa State* or *Divinity in Expression*.

The general classification of the types of meditation has been given in the above table, which serves to *summarise* the results of this chapter. Among the different kinds of meditation which are mentioned in this *Table of General Classification*,

Table of general classification

the varied forms of meditation which are resorted to before the stage of the *Sadhaka* (A), have already been illustrated in the beginning of this article. The different forms of General Meditation (B–i) will be dealt with in Part IV. The different forms of Specialised Meditation (B–ii), along with their sub-divisions, will each be explained individually in Parts V and VI. *Sahaj Samadhi* (C) and its forms will be explained in Parts VII and VIII.

The Types of Meditation

ASSIMILATION OF THE DIVINE TRUTHS

SECTION A
Modes of General Meditation

THE beginnings of spiritual life are marked and helped by general meditation, which is not concerned exclusively with selected specific items of ex-

Limits of free philosophical meditation

perience, but which, in its comprehensive scope, seeks to *understand and assimilate the Divine Truths* of life and the universe. When the aspirant is interested in the wider problems of the ultimate nature of life and the universe and begins to think about them, he may be said to have launched himself upon such meditation. *Much of what is included under philosophy is a result of trying to develop an intellectual grasp of the ultimate nature of life and the universe.* The purely intellectual grasp of Divine Truths remains feeble, incomplete and indecisive owing to the limitations of the experience which may be available as the foundation of the structures of speculation. The *philosophical meditation* of free and unaided thought does not lead to conclusive results. It often leads to diverse conflicting systems or views, but philosophical meditation is not without value. Besides leading the aspirant to a certain extent in the realm of knowledge, it gives him an intellectual discipline which enables him to receive and grasp Divine Truths when he happens to come upon them through those who *know*.

The more fruitful mode of general meditation consists in *studying the revealed Truths* concerning life and the universe. This mode of understanding and assimilating the Divine Truths can

Study of revealed truths

start from hearing or reading expositions of the Divine Truth which have their source in the Masters of Wisdom. The discourses of living Perfect Masters or the writings of the Perfect Masters of the past are a suitable object for this mode of general meditation, because the assimilation of Divine Truths, revealed through them, enables the aspirant to bring his life into line with God's purpose in the universe.

The Divine Truths are most easily grasped and assimilated when they are passed on directly to the aspirant by a living Master. Such personal communications of the Master have a

Value of hearing

power and efficacy which can never belong to information received by the aspirant through other sources. *The word becomes alive and potent because of the life and personality of the Master.* Hence many scriptures emphasise the need for *hearing* the Divine Truths directly through the spoken word of the Master (*Gurumukh*). The mode of general meditation which depends upon hearing expositions of the Divine Truths is undoubtedly the best, when the aspirant has an opportunity to contact a living Master and listen to him.

It is not always possible, however, for the aspirant to contact and listen to a living Master. In such case meditation through reading has some advantages of its

**Advantage of medita-
tion through reading**
own. For the generality of aspirants, meditation through reading has hardly any suitable substitute, because it starts from *written* expositions which are available at any convenient time. Meditation which starts from reading about revealed Truths has this special advantage of being *easily accessible* to *most aspirants*. Meditation through reading is *explained* in Section B and is *provided for* in Section C.

SECTION B

Reading as Meditation

Meditation through reading has its handicaps, because most written expositions of the Divine Truths are meant for intellectual study rather than for assimi-

**Usual handicaps in
meditation through
reading**
lation through meditation. The difficulties which aspirants experience in this connection are due either (i) to the fact that the method of meditation is not adapted to the subject-matter, or (ii) to some flaw in the method which makes it mechanical and uninspiring, or (iii) to the unwieldiness or vagueness of the subject-matter of meditation.

All these causes, which vitiate meditation and make it unsuccessful, have been avoided in the specific meditation which is recommended in this part. It is intended

**Difficulties removed
by specific meditation
through reading**
not only to explain the manner of carrying on meditation through reading, but also to provide an exposition of Divine Truth in order to fulfill the requirements of this form of meditation. The usual difficulties existing in meditation through reading have been removed in this specific meditation by (i) ensuring that *the process of meditation as well as the subject-matter are adapted to each*

other and to the conditions of intelligent meditation, (ii) by elaborately *explaining the different phases of the meditation which starts from reading*, and (iii) by *providing a specially prepared brief exposition of the Divine Truths*, which would become suitable and valuable subject matter for meditation through reading.

The form of meditation which starts from reading about the Divine Truths has three stages:

Three stages of the meditation through reading

(1) In the first stage the aspirant will have to read the exposition daily, and simultaneously think about it thoroughly.

(2) In the second stage actual reading becomes unnecessary, but the subject-matter of the exposition is mentally revived and thought over constantly.

(3) In the third stage it is quite unnecessary for the mind to revive the words in the exposition separately and consecutively, and all discursive thinking about the subject-matter comes to an end. At this stage of meditation the mind is no longer occupied with any train of thought, but has a clear, spontaneous and intuitive perception of the sublime Truth, expressed in the exposition.

Since intelligent meditation consists in *thorough thinking about a particular subject*, it follows that the best help for meditation would be a brief and clear exposition of the subject of meditation.

Subject matter for meditation through reading

The following concise exposition of the Divine Truths (given in Section C) comprises the whole story of creation, as well as a complete account of the Path and the Goal of self-realisation. The aspirant can intelligently read the exposition and assimilate the sublime truths it embodies.

This special form of meditation is extremely easy and useful, because reading the subject-matter and thinking about it have to be done simultaneously.

Advantages of specific form of meditation through reading

Further, by making the exposition of the subject-matter clear and concise, the probability of any disturbance arising out of irrelevant thoughts is eliminated. It is extremely difficult to avoid the disturbance of irrelevant thoughts while meditating upon some lengthy article or book, even if it is committed to memory. Spontaneous meditation about it therefore becomes impracticable. The appearance of irrelevant thoughts becomes very probable in lengthy meditation on abstract thoughts, or on some concrete object of experience. But irrelevant thoughts are extremely improbable if the subject-matter of meditation consists of a brief exposition of the Super-sensible Truth. If the aspirant meditates upon the following exposition of the Divine Truths in the manner which has been elaborately indicated above, meditation will become not only spontaneous and easy, delightful and inspiring, but also helpful and successful. He will thus be taking a very important step towards the realisation of the goal of life.

SECTION C

The Divine Truths

(*for meditation through reading*)

THE JOURNEY OF THE SOUL TO THE OVERSOUL

Atman or the soul is in reality identical with *Paramatman* or the Oversoul, which is One, Infinite and Eternal. The soul is, in fact, beyond the gross, subtle

The soul and its illusion

and mental worlds, but experiences itself as being limited owing to its identification with the *Sharira* or gross body, *Prana* or the subtle body (which is the vehicle of desires and vital forces), and *Manas* or the mental body (which is the seat of the mind). The soul in its transcendental state is *One—Formless, Eternal* and *Infinite*—and yet identifies itself with the phenomenal world of *forms*, which are *many* and *finite* and *destructible*. This is *Maya* or the cosmic illusion.

The phenomenal world of finite objects is *utterly illusory* and *false*. It has three states: (1) the *gross*, (2) the *subtle* and (3) the *mental*. Although all these three states of the world are false, they represent different *degrees of falseness*. Thus the gross world is farthest from Truth (God), the subtle world is nearer Truth, and the mental world is nearest to Truth. All three states of the world owe their existence to cosmic illusion which the soul has to transcend before it realises the Truth.

States of the phenomenal world

The sole purpose of creation is that the soul should be able to enjoy the infinite state of the Oversoul consciously. *Although the soul eternally exists in and with the Oversoul in an inviolable unity, it cannot be conscious of this unity independently of the creation, which is within the limitations of time.* It must therefore evolve consciousness before it can realise its true status and nature as being identical with the Infinite Oversoul, which is *One without a second*. The evolution of consciousness required the duality of subject and object—the centre of consciousness and the environment (*i. e.*, the world of forms).

Purpose of creation

How does the soul get caught up in the illusion? How did the Formless, Infinite and Eternal Soul come to experience itself as having form, and as being finite and destructible? How did *Purusha* or the Supreme

Genesis of cosmic illusion

Spirit come to think of itself as *Prakriti* or the world of nature? In other words, what is the cause of the cosmic illusion in which the soul finds itself?

To realise the true status of the Oversoul which is One, Indivisible, Real and Infinite, the soul needed consciousness. The soul did get consciousness, but this consciousness was not of *God* but of the *universe;* not of the *Oversoul* but of its *shadow;* not of the *One* but of many; not of the *Infinite* but of the *finite;* not of the *Eternal* but of the *transitory.* Thus the soul, instead of realising the Oversoul, gets involved in the cosmic illusion, and hence, though really infinite, it comes to experience itself as finite. In other words, *when the soul develops consciousness it does not become conscious of its own true nature but of the phenomenal world*, which is its own shadow.

In order to become conscious of the phenomenal world the soul must assume some form (as its medium) for experiencing the world, and the degree and kind of

Organic evolution and degrees of consciousness

consciousness are determined by the nature of the form which is used as a medium. The soul first becomes conscious of the gross world by assuming a gross body. The consciousness of the gross world which it has in the beginning is of the most partial and rudimentary type. Correspondingly the soul assumes the most undeveloped form (*e. g.*, that of stone), with which evolution begins. *The driving force of evolution is constituted by the momentum which consciousness receives owing to the conservation of the impressions (sanskaras) left by diverse desires or conditions.* Thus the *sanskaras* cultivated in a particular form have to be worked out and fulfilled through the medium of *a higher* form and a correspondingly more developed consciousness of the gross world. The soul, therefore, has to assume higher and higher forms (like metal, vegetable, worm, fish, bird and animal) until at last it assumes a human form, in which it has developed *full consciousness* (in all the aspects of knowing, feeling and willing) of the gross world.

The manner in which *sanskaras* result in the evolution of consciousness and the corresponding form has a useful analogue in ordinary experience. If a man has

Driving force of evolution

the desire to act the part of a king on the stage he can only experience it by actually putting on the garb of a king and going to the stage. This is true of aspirations and desires, which can only be worked out and fulfilled by bringing about an actual change in the entire situation, as well as the medium, through which the situation may be adequately experienced. The parallel is very suggestive in understanding the driving force of evolution, which *is not mechanical but purposive.*

The *sanskaras* are not only responsible for *the evolution of the form* (body) and the kind of consciousness connected with it, but they are also responsible for *the*

Identification with form

riveting of consciousness to the phenomenal world. They make emancipation of consciousness (*i. e.*, the withdrawal of consciousness from the phenomenal world to the soul itself) impossible at the sub-human stage and difficult at the human level. Since consciousness clings to the previous *sanskaras*, and experience of the phenomenal world is conditioned by the use of an adequate form (body) as a medium, the soul at every stage of evolution comes to *identify itself with the form* (*e. g.*, stone, metal, vegetable, animal, etc.).

Thus the soul, which in reality is infinite and formless, experiences itself as finite and thinks of itself as being a stone, metal, vegetable, worm, fish, bird or animal, *according to the degree* of the development of consciousness. Finally, *while experiencing the gross world through the human form, the soul thinks that it is a human being.*

The soul has developed *full* consciousness in the human form, and therefore there is no need for any further evolution of the gross form (body). The evolu-

Reincarnation and the law of *karma*

tion of forms, therefore, comes to an end with the attainment of the human form; and to experience the *sanskaras* cultivated in the human form, the soul has to *reincarnate* again and again in human forms. The innumerable human forms, through which the soul has to pass, are determined by the law of *karma*, or the nature of its previous *sanskaras* (*i. e.*, whether of virtue or vice, happiness or misery). During these lives the soul, which is eternal, *identifies itself with the gross body*, which is destructible.

While developing full consciousness of the gross world in the human form, the soul *simultaneously* develops the subtle and mental bodies; but as long as its

Subtle and mental bodies

consciousness is confined to the gross world alone, it cannot use these bodies *consciously* in wakefulness. It becomes conscious of these bodies and the corresponding worlds only when its full consciousness turns *inwards*, *i. e.*, towards itself. When the soul is conscious of the subtle world through the subtle body, it identifies itself with the subtle body, and when it is conscious of the mental world through the mental body, it identifies itself with the mental body, just as it identifies itself with the gross body when it is conscious of the gross world through the gross body.

The homeward journey of the soul consists in freeing itself from the illusion of being identical with its bodies—gross, subtle and mental. When the atten-

The Path

tion of the soul turns towards self-knowledge and self-real-isation, there is a gradual loosening and disappearance of the *sanskaras* which keep consciousness turned towards the phenomenal world. *Disappearance of the sanskaras proceeds side by side with piercing through the veil of cosmic illusion,* and the soul not only begins to transcend the different states of the phenomenal world, but also to know itself as different from its bodies. The Path begins when the soul tries to find itself and turns its full consciousness towards Truth (God).

At the first stage the soul becomes totally unconscious of its gross body and of the gross world, and experiences the *subtle* world through the medium of its subtle body, with which it identifies itself. In the second stage the soul is totally unconscious of its gross and subtle bodies, and also of the gross and subtle worlds, and experiences the *mental* world through the medium of its mental body with which it now identifies itself. At this stage the soul may be said to be *face to face with God or the Oversoul,* which it recognises as Infinite. But though it recognises the Infinity of the Oversoul, which it *objectifies,* it looks upon itself as being finite because of its identification with the mind or mental body.

Thus we have the *paradox* that *the soul, which in reality is infinite, sees its infinite state but still continues to regard itself as finite, because while seeing its infinite state, it looks upon itself as the mind.* It imagines itself to be the mind and looks upon the object of the mind as the Oversoul. Further, it not only longs to be one with the objectified Oversoul but also tries hard to fulfill that longing.

In the third stage the full consciousness of the soul is drawn still further inwards (*i. e.*, towards itself) and it ceases to identify itself even with the mental body.

The Goal   Thus in the third and last stage (which is the goal), the soul *ceases to identify itself with any of the three bodies* which it had to develop for evolving full consciousness. Now it not only knows itself to be formless and beyond all the bodies and worlds, but also realises with full consciousness its own unity with the Oversoul, which is One, Indivisible, Real and Infinite. In this realisation of the Truth it enjoys infinite bliss, peace, power and knowledge, which are characteristics of the Oversoul.

In the beginning, because it had not evolved consciousness, the soul was unconscious of its identity with the Oversoul, and hence, though part and parcel of

Summary   the Oversoul, it could not realise its own identity with it or experience infinite peace, bliss, power and knowledge. Even after the evolution of consciousness it could not realise the state of the Oversoul (although it is all the time in and with the Oversoul) because its consciousness is confined to the phenomenal world owing to the *sanskaras* connected with the evolution of consciousness. Even on the Path, the soul is not conscious of itself, but is conscious only of the gross, subtle and mental worlds which are its own illusory shadows. At the end of the Path, however, *the soul frees itself from all sanskaras and desires connected with the gross, subtle and mental worlds; and it becomes possible for it to free itself from the illusion of being finite, which came into existence owing to its identification with the gross, subtle and mental bodies*. At this stage the soul completely transcends the phenomenal world and becomes *Self-conscious and Self-realised*. For attaining this goal, the soul must retain its full consciousness and at the same time know itself to be different from the *Sharira* (gross body), *Prana* (subtle body, which is the vehicle of desires and vital forces) and *Manas* (mental body, which is the seat of the mind), and also as being *beyond* the gross, subtle and mental worlds.

The soul has to emancipate itself gradually from the illusion of being finite by (1) *liberating itself from the bondage of sanskaras*, and (2) *knowing itself to be different from its bodies*—gross, subtle and mental. It thus annihilates the *false ego* (*i. e.*, the illusion that "I am the gross body, I am the subtle body or I am the mental body"). While the soul thus frees itself from its illusion, it still retains full consciousness, which now results in Self-knowledge and realisation of the Truth. *Escaping through the cosmic illusion and realising with full consciousness its identity with the Infinite Oversoul, is the goal of the long journey of the soul.*

The Types of Meditation

IT was seen in Part III that specialised meditation is of three kinds: (i) meditation concerned with the *objects* of experience, (ii) meditation concerned with the

Kinds of specialised meditation

subject of experience, and (iii) meditation concerned with *mental operations*. These three *kinds of meditation are mostly intertwined with each other*, because the subject of experience, the objects of experience and the different mental operations which arise as a result of their interaction, are all inextricably interwoven with each other. So these three kinds of meditation are not sharply defined or exclusive, but often overlap each other. Thus, meditation concerned with the objects of experience may often refer to the subject of experience, and also to the diverse mental operations involved in it. Meditation concerned with the subject of experience may often involve reference to the diverse mental operations and the objects to which these mental operations are directed. And meditation concerned with the diverse mental operations may often involve reference to both the subject and the objects of experience. Yet each kind of meditation, in a way, remains distinct because of some *predominating* factor. Thus the first kind of meditation remains predominantly concerned with the *objects of experience*, the second kind with the *subject of experience* and the *third*

Table of Enumerative Classification of the Forms of Specialised Meditation

A	Meditation concerned with the *objects* of experience	1	Meditation on the divine qualities of the Master	**FORMS OF PERSONAL MEDITATION**
		2	Concentration on the *form* of the Master	
		3	The Meditation of the *heart*	
		4	The Meditation of *action*	
		5	Meditation regarding the numerous forms of manifested life	**FORMS OF IMPERSONAL MEDITATION**
		6	Meditation regarding one's own bodies	
		7	Meditation on the *formless and infinite aspect of God*	
B	Meditation concerned with the *subject* of experience	8	Quest for the *agent* of action	
		9	Considering oneself as the *witness*	
C	Meditation concerned with *mental* operations	10	Writing down thoughts	
		11	Watching mental operations	
		12	Making the mind *blank*	

kind with the diverse *mental operations*.

These three kinds of meditation can each be further subdivided into numerous specific forms of meditation according to the content of the meditation and

Table of enumerative classification

the manner in which it is conducted. Out of these numerous forms of specialised meditation only those which are *representative* or *important* need particular mention. Thus *twelve* forms of specialised meditation are given on page 147.

It should be noted that of these twelve forms of specialised meditation, mentioned in *the Table of Enumerative Classification*, the first four are forms of *Personal*

Personal meditation and impersonal meditation

Meditation and the remaining eight are forms of *Impersonal Meditation*. Meditation is personal when it is concerned with a person, and meditation is impersonal when it is concerned with (*a*) aspects of human personality or (*b*) something which falls outside the range of human personality as it is usually understood. The forms of specialised meditation which are personal will be explained individually within this Part, and the forms of specialised meditation which are impersonal will be explained individually in Part VI.

Personal meditation has some clear advantages over impersonal meditation. For beginners, personal meditation is easy and attended with joy, while imper-

Special advantages of personal meditation

sonal meditation is often found dry and difficult unless one has a special aptitude for it. Moreover, forms of impersonal meditation are mostly disciplines for the mind or the intellect, but the forms of personal meditation are not only disciplines for the mind or the intellect but also draw out the heart. In spiritual perfection the mind and the heart have to be fully developed and balanced. Therefore personal meditation, which helps the development and balancing of the mind and the heart, has special importance. Impersonal meditation is really fruitful and effective when the aspirant has been duly prepared through forms of personal meditation.

Personal meditation is directed towards *persons who are spiritually perfect*. Just as a man who admires the character of Napoleon and constantly thinks about him

Personal meditation directed towards spiritually perfect persons

has a tendency to become like him, so an aspirant who admires some spiritually perfect person and constantly thinks about him has a tendency to become spiritually perfect. A suitable object for personal meditation is *a living Master or Avatar* or *Masters and Avatars of the past.* It is important that the object of meditation be spiritually perfect. *If the person selected for meditation happens to be spiritually imperfect, there is every chance of his frailties percolating into the mind of the aspirant who meditates upon him.* If the person selected for meditation is spiritually perfect, however, the aspirant has taken to a safe and sure path.

Personal meditation often begins with the admiration which an aspirant feels spontaneously for some divine quality which he sees in the Master. *By allowing*

Meditation on divine qualities of Master

the mind to dwell upon the divine qualities expressed in the life of the Master, the aspirant imbibes them into his own being[1]. Ultimately, the Master, on his part, is beyond all qualities—good and bad. He is not bound by them. The qualities which he exhibits, while interacting with life around, are all different aspects of

---

[1] Meditation No. 1, *Table of Enumerative Classification.*

divinity in action; and the expression of divinity, through qualities, becomes a medium for helping those who are appreciatively responsive to them. Appreciation of the divinity perceived in the Master gives rise to forms of meditation in which the aspirant constantly and strenuously thinks of the Master as being an embodiment of qualities like universal love or complete detachment, egolessness or steadfastness, infinite knowledge or selfless action. Sometimes the mind may dwell upon such separate qualities or may dwell upon combined qualities which reveal their inter-relatedness. This form of meditation is very valuable when it is spontaneous. *It then leads to a greater understanding of the Master and gradually remoulds the aspirant into a likeness of the Master*, thus contributing towards his self-preparation for the realisation of the Truth.

Dwelling upon the qualities of the Master often facilitates *concentration* on the *form* of the Master[2]. In this form of meditation, the aspirant is aware of the

Concentration on form of Master

spiritual perfection of the Master and spontaneously fixes his attention upon the form of the Master *without analysing his spiritual perfection into any of its component qualities*. However, though these qualities are not separately revived in the mind, all that the aspirant may have understood of them (through the preparatory meditation concerned with the diverse qualities of the Master) constitutes the *implicit* background of such one-pointed concentration, and contributes towards its efficacy and value. This form of meditation involves complete identification of the Master with the spiritual ideal.

Complete identification of the Master with the spiritual ideal is responsible for removing such barriers

---

[2] Meditation No. 2, *Table of Enumerative Classification*.

as might exist between the aspirant and the Master.

Meditation of the heart

This gives rise to the release of unrestrained love for the Master and leads to the *meditation of the heart*[3], which consists in constant thinking about the Master with uninterrupted flow of limitless love. Such love annihilates the illusion of separateness, which seems to divide the aspirant from the Master, and it has in it a *spontaneity which is virtually without parallel in other forms of meditation*. In its final stages, meditation of the heart is accompanied by unbounded joy and utter forgetfulness of self.

Love for the Master leads to increasing identification with the Master, so that the aspirant desires to *live in and for the Master and not for his own narrow self*.

Modes of meditation of action

This leads to the *meditation of action*[4]. The initial modes of the meditation of action usually take the following forms: (*a*) The aspirant *mentally offers the Master all that is in him*, thus renouncing all that is good or evil in him. This frees him from the good as well as the bad ingredients of the ego and helps him not only in *transcending these opposites*, but also in *finding a lasting and true integration with the Master*. (*b*) The aspirant volunteers himself in the service of the Master or his cause. Doing work for the Master in the spirit of selfless service is as good as meditation. (*c*) The aspirant does not allow the ego to feed upon any of his actions—small or great, good or bad. He does not think "I do this," but on the contrary, systematically develops the thought that through him the Master is really doing all that he does. For example, when he looks, he thinks, "The Master is looking;" when he eats, he thinks,

---

[3] Meditation No. 3, *Table of Enumerative Classification*.

[4] Meditation No. 4, *Table of Enumerative Classification*.

"The Master is eating;" when he sleeps, he thinks, "The Master is sleeping;" when he drives a car, he thinks, "The Master is driving the car;" even when he may happen to do something wrong, he thinks, "The Master is doing this." Thus he completely relinquishes all agency for his action, and all that is done by him is brought into direct reference to the Master. This automatically and necessarily involves and entails *determination of each action in the light of the spiritual ideal as seen in the Master.*

The four forms of personal meditation on the Master represent the four main *ascending stages:* (i) *perceiving* the spiritual ideal in the Master, (ii) *concentrating* upon the Master as an embodiment of the spiritual ideal, (iii) *loving* the Master as a manifestation of the spiritual ideal, and (iv) *expressing* the spiritual ideal, perceived in the Master, in one's own life. Personal meditation on the Master, in its different forms, ultimately contributes towards the release of *creative life of spiritual fulfillment.* Meditation on the Master is a meditation on *the living ideal* and not on the bare conception of perfection. Therefore it generates that dynamic power which eventually enables the aspirant to bridge over the gulf between theory and practice, and unify the spiritual ideal with everyday activity in his own life. *To live a life inspired and illumined by the spiritual ideal, as embodied in the Master, is the culmination of all the forms of personal meditation.*

Four forms of personal meditation represent four ascending stages

The Types of Meditation

PART VI
SPECIALISED MEDITATIONS WHICH ARE IMPERSONAL

PART V was devoted to explanatory comments on those specialised meditations which are personal. This part will be devoted to those specialised medita-

Distinction between personal and impersonal meditation

tions which are impersonal. It might be recalled that meditation is personal when it is concerned with a person, and impersonal when it is concerned with (a) aspects of personality or (b) something which falls outside the range of human personality, as it is commonly understood. In the *Table of Enumerative Classification* given in Part V, the first four forms of meditation are personal and the remaining eight forms are impersonal. Like the forms of personal meditation, the forms of impersonal meditation also individually deserve separate explanatory comments.

Man's attention has a tendency to be riveted on his own bodies or on other forms independent of the spirit which they manifest. This leads to illusions, entanglements and other complications. Hence arises the need for a type of meditation which will enable

Meditation regarding numerous forms of manifested life

the aspirant to develop *proper perspective* concerning the real status and meaning of the numerous forms, and to cultivate a *right attitude* to them[1]. In this type of meditation the aspirant acquires the constant habit *of regarding all forms as equally the manifestations of the same one all-pervading life and as nothing in themselves separately.* This type of meditation aids *disentanglement from the world of creation,* and furthers cultivation of the highest type of *universal love, which regards the whole of humanity and all living creatures as members of an indivisible whole.*

But the type of meditation which is concerned with the numerous forms of manifested life remains incomplete unless it is supplemented by another type of medi-

Meditation regarding one's bodies

tation which is concerned with one's own body[2]. One's own body—gross, subtle or mental —is, like the bodies of others, a form of the one all-pervading life; but consciousness is fixed on one's own bodies by *an attachment so deep that it identifies itself with them.* Continued thoughts of detachment concerning one's own body help emancipation of consciousness and the dawn of true self-knowedge. Meditation of this type is very fruitful for the aspirant. The gross, subtle and mental bodies are all then regarded as cloaks which one can put on or off.

The type of meditation concerned with the numerous forms of manifested life and the type of meditation concerned with one's own bodies, are both preparations for the form of impersonal meditation[3] in which (*a*) an effort is made to *withdraw* consciousness

---

[1] Meditation No. 5, *Table of Enumerative Classification* (Part V).

[2] Meditation No. 6, *Table of Enumerative Classification* (Part V).

[3] Meditation No. 7, *Table of Enumerative Classification* (Part V).

Meditation on formless and infinite aspect of God

from all the numerous forms of manifested life as well as from one's own bodies, and (b) *to centre consciousness on the formless and infinite aspect* of God. In the initial phases, this form of impersonal meditation has to avail itself of some *symbols of infinity*. It is actually more helpful to start with some *image* which suggests and signifies infinity than the *abstract idea* of infinity. The mind may be made steady on the image of sky, ocean or vast emptiness, but when once a particular image is chosen, the aspirant should stick to it throughout the period of meditation, and not allow it to be replaced by another image. Out of these symbols of infinity, complete and unlimited emptiness is difficult to imagine, but it turns out to be the best symbol if one can successfully bring it before one's mind. Even when unlimited emptiness is used to signify infinity, in this form of meditation the aspirant is not supposed to arrive at complete blankness of mind. Such blankness involves the cessation of all mental activity and having absolutely no thoughts or ideas; but in this form of meditation the mind tries to understand and realise the formless and infinite aspect of God by means of a significant symbol.

There is an important variety of this impersonal form of meditation. In it the infinity which one imagines is not mentally externalised as if it were an unlimited

Picturing the infinite as being within

stretch of something *outside* the aspirant. It is more helpful to picture the infinite as *within* the aspirant. After picturing infinity within, the aspirant should give himself the strong suggestion of his identity with the infinite by mentally repeating, "I am as infinite as the sky within," or "I am as infinite as the ocean within," or "I am as infinite as the emptiness within." It may be even more useful to use the bare formula, "I am the Infinite within" and, while mentally repeating this formula, to grasp and realise the significance of infinity through the image which has been chosen. It is not necessary to repeat the formula in so many *words;* it is enough to cling to the *thought* expressed in the formula.

The "I am infinite" meditation may lead to the merging of the aspirant into the formless and infinite aspect of God. Some aspirants merge so completely that even if swarms of mosquitoes pass by them they do not hear them. Some aspirants might become restless or easily disturbed. They should not keep worrying about lack of success in meditation but should tenaciously persist whether they experience merging or not. A relaxed position is helpful for merging, but a final merging is impossible except through the help of the Master.

The forms of meditation thus far explained are predominantly concerned with the impersonal *objects* of experience, but some impersonal forms of meditation are concerned with the *subject* of experience. One such important form of meditation consists in ceaselessly pressing the query, "Who is it that does all these things?"[4] The aspirant finds himself thinking thoughts like, "I sleep," "I walk," "I eat," "I talk," "I see, hear, touch, taste and smell," "I think, feel and desire," etc. Now the searching question with which this form of meditation is concerned, is "WHO IS THIS 'I'?" *The soul does not experience any of these things.* The soul does not sleep, walk, eat or talk, see, hear, touch, taste or smell, think, feel or desire. Who then is their agent? The *source* of all these activities has to be

Quest for agent of action

---

[4] Meditation No. 8, *Table of Enumerative Classification* (Part V).

discovered and the mystery of all life has to be explained.

There is a power that does all these things, and one must *know* oneself to be different from the power and be able to use it with detachment. The aspirant *thinks* that he walks; it is really his *body* that walks. The aspirant *thinks* that he sees, hears, thinks, feels or desires; it is really his *mind* which does all these things through some convenient medium. *As soul, the aspirant is everywhere and really does nothing.* But it is not enough to think that as soul he is everywhere and really does nothing. He must *know* this.

Knowledge of the soul may also be aimed at through a form of meditation in which the aspirant tries to realise himself as merely a *witness of all physical and mental happenings*[5]. After a person wakes from a dream, he realises that he was not a real *agent* of the actions in the dream, but that he was merely a *witness* of them. If the aspirant persistently practises considering himself a witness of all physical and mental happenings which he experiences in wakefulness as well as in dreams, he soon develops *utter detachment*, which brings freedom from all worries and sufferings connected with worldly events. This form of meditation is intended to lift the aspirant *out of the bonds of time*, and to secure for him immediate relief from the fret and fever connected with the diverse expressions of limited energy. *As a witness, the soul remains aloof from all events in time, and the results of actions do not bind it.* All this has to be *experienced* and not merely thought of.

Considering oneself as the witness

The forms of meditation concerned with the subject of experience, however, suffer from the handicap that *the true subject of experience can never be the object of*

---

[5] Meditation No. 9, *Table of Enumerative Classification (Part V).*

Importance of making the mind still

thought or meditation in the ordinary sense. These forms of meditation, therefore, can at best take the aspirant very close to self-knowledge which can only dawn in its full glory when the domain of the mind is completely traversed. Some impersonal forms of specialised meditation are therefore concerned with *mental operations*, and they ultimately aim at *stilling the mind*.

To acquire control over thoughts is to become fully conscious of what they are. They have to be attended to before they are controlled. In ordinary introspection it

Writing down thoughts

is seldom possible for the beginner to devote adequate attention to all the shadowy thoughts which pass through his mind. It is helpful, therefore, for the aspirant occasionally to write down all his thoughts[6] as they come and then to inspect them carefully at leisure. This process is different from writing planned articles. Thoughts are allowed to arise without any direction or restraint so that even repressed elements from the subconscious mind have access to the conscious mind.

In a more advanced stage, an intensive awareness of mental processes can take place while thoughts appear in consciousness, and writing them down be-

Watching mental operations

comes unnecessary. Observation of mental operations[7] should be accompanied by critical evaluation of thoughts. Thoughts cannot be controlled except through an appreciation of their value or lack of value. When the diverse thoughts which assail the mind are critically evaluated, and the internal

---

[6] Meditation No. 10, *Table of Enumerative Classification* (Part V).
[7] Meditation No. 11, *Table of Enumerative Classification* (Part V).

stirrings of *sanskaras* are faced, understood and taken for what they are worth, the mind is freed from all obsessions and compulsions in relation to them.

A way is thus prepared for the meditation which attempts to make the mind blank[8], which is one of the most difficult things to achieve. *The mind is without any*

Making the mind blank

ideas during sleep, but consciousness is then in abeyance. If during wakefulness the mind has the idea of becoming blank, it is thinking about that idea and is far from being blank. But this difficult trick of making the mind blank becomes possible by an *alternation* between two incompatible forms of meditation so that the mind is *caught between concentration and distraction.*

Thus the aspirant can concentrate on the Master for five minutes and then, as the mind is getting settled on the form of the Master, he can steady his mind for

Alternation between concentration and distraction

the next five minutes in the impersonal meditation in which the thought is "I am Infinite." The disparity between the two forms of meditation can be emphasised by keeping the eyes open during meditation on the form of the Master, and closing the eyes during impersonal meditation. Such alternation helps towards making the mind blank, but to be successful, both forms of meditation have to be seriously pursued. Though after five minutes there is to be a change-over to another type of meditation, there should be no thought of it while the first type is going on. There is no distraction unless there is concentration. But when a change-over is effected, there should be no thought of the first type of meditation. The distraction has to be as complete as the previous concentration. *When there is a quick alterna-*

---

[8] Meditation No. 12, *Table of Enumerative Classification* (Part V).

tion between concentration and distraction, mental operations are, as it were, cut through by a saw which goes backwards and forwards. The disappearance of mental operations of all types contributes towards making the mind absolutely still without allowing consciousness to fall into abeyance.

All thoughts which appear in the mind of the aspirant are forms of perturbation, and have their origin in the momentum of stored *sanskaras*. The agitation of the mind can disappear only when the aspirant can so control his mind that all thoughts can be ruled out at will. *Only in complete internal silence is Truth found.* When the surface of the lake is still, it reflects the stars. *When the mind is tranquil, it reflects the nature of the soul as it is.*

Truth reflected in the mind which becomes tranquil

The Types of Meditation

PART VII
SAHAJ SAMADHI

THE different forms of meditation practised before consciously entering the Path, as well as the different forms of general and special meditation

**Sahaj Samadhi
stands by itself**

adopted after becoming an aspirant, are preparatory to the attainment of the highest state of *Sahaj Samadhi* or spontaneous meditation, in which the aspirant becomes permanently established when he realises the ultimate goal of life. The *Sahaj Samadhi* of the *Siddha* or God-realised person is *continuous* with all the prior forms of meditation and is a *culmination* of them, but different in kind, and belongs to an *entirely different order*.

The spontaneity or effortlessness of *Sahaj Samadhi* must be carefully distinguished from the pseudo-sense of spontaneity which is present in the usual meditations

**Pre-spiritual
meditations of
worldly man**

of the worldly man who has not yet entered the Path. The mind of the worldly man is engrossed in the object of sense, and he experiences no sense of effort in meditating on these objects. His mind dwells upon them because of its natural interest in them and not because of any deliberate effort on his part. The sense of effort does not arise from allowing the mind to dwell upon these diverse worldly objects, but from trying to dissuade it from them. So the pre-spiritual forms of meditation seem to have some similarity with the culminating *Sahaj Samadhi* of the *Siddha*, in having a sense of spontaneity. But this resemblance between the initial phase of meditation and its final phase is only superficial, since *Sahaj Samadhi* and pre-spiritual meditations are divided from each other by vital differences of great spiritual importance.

The sense of spontaneity experienced in pre-spiritual meditations concerned with worldly objects and pursuits, is due to the interests created by *sanskaras*.

Illusory spontaneity of pre-spiritual meditations derived from *sanskaric* interests

Pre-spiritual meditations are the working out of the momentum of accumulated sanskaras of the past; and they are not only far from being the expression of true freedom, but are actually symptoms of spiritual bondage. At the pre-spiritual level, man is engulfed in unrelieved ignorance concerning the goal of infinite freedom; and though he is far from being happy and contented, he identifies so deeply with *sanskaric interests* that he experiences gratification in their furtherance. But the pleasure of his pursuits is conditional and transitory, and the *spontaneity which he experiences in them is illusory* because, through all his pursuits, his mind is working under limitations.

The mind is capable of genuine freedom and spontaneity of action only when it is completely free from *sanskaric* ties and interests, and this is possible only when it is merged in the state of *Sahaj Samadhi* of the *Siddha*. It is therefore important to note that

True freedom and spontaneity exist only in *Sahaj Samadhi* though there may seem to be a superficial resemblance between the *Sahaj Samadhi* of the *Siddha* and the pre-spiritual meditations of the worldly man, this resemblance really hides the important difference between illusory spontaneity and true spontaneity, bondage and freedom, fleeting pleasure and abiding happiness. *In the pre-spiritual meditations the movement of the mind is under unconscious compulsion, and in Sahaj Samadhi mental activity is released under conscious and unfettered initiative.*

The different forms of meditation which characterise the life of the spiritual aspirant, stand *midway* between the pre-spiritual meditations of the worldly

Meditation a part of aspirant's struggle towards emancipation man and the final *Sahaj Samadhi* of the *Siddha*. They also constitute the link between them. When man's primary acquiescence in *sanskaric* interests is profoundly disturbed by setback, defeat and suffering, or is shaken by a spark of spiritual understanding, he becomes conscious of his bondage and the falseness of his perceptions. *All the different forms of meditation which are then resorted to by the aspirant arise as parts of his struggle towards emancipation from the bondage of the deceptive desires of the worldly man.* The forms of meditation which are spiritually important begin when a person has become an aspirant or *Sadhaka*.

The meditation of the aspirant in all its forms is *deliberate*, in the sense that it is experienced as counteracting instinctive or other tendencies inherent in the

Meditation involves effort mind. The aspirant adopts different forms of meditation as a means to an end, *i.e.*, because he looks upon them as avenues to the Truth.

They are not a working out of some given impulse, but are parts of an intelligent and deliberate effort. But, though these forms of meditation may be deliberate to start with, the mind gradually becomes habituated to them. The mind is also interested in the various aspects of Truth, which the different forms of meditation try to seize upon, and this increases spontaneity. In none of the meditations of a *sadhaka* is the element of spontaneity more pronounced than in those forms of personal meditation which give scope for and require the expression of love. But utter spontaneity and true freedom remain unattained until the goal of meditation is achieved. Till then there is usually a mixture of a sense of deliberateness and a sense of spontaneity. The reaching out towards spiritual freedom is accompanied throughout by a sense of effort, which persists in some degree until all obstacles of false perceptions are overcome. *Though effort may vary in its intensity, it never disappears entirely until it is swallowed up in the tranquillity of final attainment.*

In *Sahaj Samadhi* there is no effort because there are no obstacles to overcome or objectives to achieve. There is the *infinite spontaneity of unfettered freedom and*

Progression towards Sahaj Samadhi

the unbroken peace and bliss of Truth-Realisation. Progression towards *Sahaj Samadhi* consists in a transition from a state of unquestioned acquiescence in the momentum of *sanskaras* to a state of desperate struggle with *sanskaric* limitations and finally to a state of complete freedom, *when consciousness is no longer determined by the deposits of the past, but is active in the undimmed perception of the eternal Truth.*

The *Sahaj Samadhi* of the *Siddha* is different from the meditation of the aspirant, not only with respect to freedom and spontaneity of consciousness, but also

Only in *Sahaj Sama-dhi* **is individual mind merged** with respect to many other important points. All the different forms of meditation in which the aspirant might be engaged, directly or indirectly, aim at securing a complete merging of the mind in the infinite Truth, but they only partially succeed in merging and fall short of the annihilation of the individual mind. They represent varying degrees of approximation to the spiritual goal, but not its realisation. On the other hand, in *Sahaj Samadhi* there is realisation of the spiritual goal, since the limited mind is completely annihilated and has arrived at a total merging in the infinite Truth.

The aspirant's meditation, in its higher flights, often brings to him a sense of expansion and freedom, as well as the joy and illumination of the higher planes, **Temporary exalta-tion in meditation** but none of these are abiding because *in most cases when the aspirant comes down from his exalted state of meditation he is again what he was, viz.,* an ordinary person who is held up in the unyielding shackles of *sanskaric* limitations.

The incompleteness of the different *samadhis* of the aspirant may be illustrated by the story of a *Yogi* from Gwalior. This *Yogi* was very greedy, but through **Story of a Yogi** *yoga* he had mastered the art of going into *samadhi*. One day he sat opposite the palace of the Raja and, before going into *samadhi*, thought, "I must have a thousand rupees from the Raja." Then he went into *samadhi* and remained in that state for seven full days. During this period he took no food or drink, but only sat in one place, completely wrapped up in *trance-meditation*. People took him to be a saint, and when the Raja came to know about him he also went to have his *darshan*. The Raja went near the *Yogi* and happened to touch him on his back. That light touch was sufficient to bring the *Yogi* down from his *samadhi*, and as soon as he woke up from his trance-meditation he asked the Raja for a thousand rupees.

Just as a prisoner, who looks out of the window of his prison and gazes at the vast expanse of the sky, may get lost in the vision of unlimited space, the aspirant who enters into trance-meditation may temporarily forget all his limitations while immersed in its light and bliss. But though the prisoner may have forgotten the prison, he has not escaped from it. In the same way *the aspirant who is absorbed in trance-meditation has lost sight of the chains which bind him to the world of Illusion, but he has not really broken through them.* Just as the prisoner again becomes conscious of his bondage as soon as he gazes at his immediate surroundings, so the aspirant becomes conscious of all his failings as soon as he regains normal consciousness. The ascending forms of trance-meditation may bring to the aspirant increasing occult *powers*, but not that unending state of knowlege and bliss which is continuously accessible in *Sahaj Samadhi* to the *Siddha*, who has attained final emancipation by breaking through the chains of *Maya*.

Analysis of trance-meditation

Another important difference is that in trance-meditation the aspirant is usually *sustained by some phenomenal object* capable of exercising irresistible attraction. The lights, colours, smells and sounds of the *subtle sphere* play a part in alluring the mind from worldly things to which it may have been attached. Thus trance-me-

Trance-meditation sustained by phenomenal object

ditation is not self-sustained but is dependent upon the object to which the mind directs itself.

The Sahaj Samadhi of the Siddha is self-sustained and is in no way dependent upon any object of the mind. Trance-meditation is more like the *stupor of intoxicating drugs.*

Sahaj Samadhi self-sustained

The intoxication of the drug lasts only as long as the effect of the drug lasts. So the trance continues to exist as long as the mind is under the sway of the object by which it is sustained. *Sahaj Samadhi* which is free from the domination of the object is *a state of full wakefulness in which there is no ebb and flow, waxing or waning, but only the steadiness of true perception.*

The different forms of general and specialised meditation resorted to by the aspirant are *useful and valuable within their own limits.* They must not be regarded

Those in *Sahaj Sama-dhi* are proper objects for meditation

as having the same value for all or as being equally neces-sary to all. They are among the ways which lead the as-pirant towards his divine destination. For the few who are in an advanced spiritual state, most of the ordinary forms of meditation are unnecessary. For those who are in direct contact with a God-realised Master, many of the special forms of meditation are often unnecessary. It is enough for them to be under the guidance of the Master and to love him. And those rare beings who have attained Self-realisation and are always in the state of *Sahaj Samadhi*, not only do not need any forms of meditation, but they *themselves become objects of meditation* for the aspirants; for they are then able to give their best help to those who meditate upon them.

The Types of Meditation

PART VIII
THE ASCENT TO SAHAJ SAMADHI
AND ITS NATURE

WHEN the mind is rightly tuned to the object of meditation, it merges in the Truth and experiences *Sahaj Samadhi* or state of spontaneous enjoyment of

Sahaj Samadhi culmination of earlier forms of meditation

uninterrupted Self-knowledge in which the aspirant loses his limited individuality to discover that he is identical with God, Who is in everything. *Sahaj Samadhi* is a *culmination* of the earlier forms of personal and impersonal meditation and not their *product.*

All forms of meditation followed by the aspirant, as well as his other spiritual efforts, in spite of their differences, have only one aim., *viz.*, to speed up the

Sahaj Samadhi experienced after union with the Infinite

fruition of his longing to be united with the Infinite. When this union is effected, the *Sadhaka* (aspirant) becomes *Siddha* (one who has attained the goal). The union with the Infinite which the *Siddha* achieves is referred to by the Sufis as "*Vasl.*" It is this state of union with God which is described by Christ in the words, "*I and my Father are one.*" Many have written about this highest state of consciousness, but it remains essentially indescribable. It cannot be expressed in words, and therefore it cannot be adequately explained. But *though it can never be explained by one person to another, it can be experienced by everyone for himself.* This highest state of the *Siddha* is called *Sahaj Samadhi.*

To dwell in *Sahaj Samadhi* is to experience the *God-state* in which the soul knows itself to be God, because it has shed all the limiting factors which had hitherto contributed towards false self-knowledge. The *God-state* of

Life of the body

the *Siddha* stands out in clear contrast with the *body-state* of the worldly man. The worldly man takes himself to be the body, and dwells in a state which is dominated by the body and its wants. His consciousness centres on the body. He is concerned with eating, drinking, sleeping and the satisfaction of other bodily desires. *It is for the body that he lives and seeks fulfillment.* His consciousness cannot extend beyond the body; he thinks in terms of the body and cannot think of anything which has no body or form. *The entire sphere of his existence is conprised of forms,* and the theatre in which he lives and moves and has his being consists of space.

The first step towards the *God-state* of *Sahaj Samadhi* is taken when the body-state is transcended. Shedding the body-state means entering the sphere of existence which is comprised of energy.

Life of energy

The soul then dwells in a state which is no longer dominated by forms or bodies. It is lifted up to the domain of energy. *Body or form is a solidification of energy, and to rise from the world of forms to the sphere of energy amounts to an advance towards a more primary and purer state of being. The energy-state* is free from many of the limitations which obtain in the world of forms. In this state, consciousness is linked up with energy and continuously vibrates in and through energy. In the energy-state, the eating and drinking of the body-state are paralleled by the absorption and assimilation of energy. At this level the soul acquires full control over energy and seeks fulfillment through its use. But its actions are still within the domain of spiritual limitation. It can see, hear and smell many things which are inaccessible in the body-state, and can perform many things (*e. g.*, producing light in the dark, or living for thousands of years only on the drinking of energy), which seem to be *miracles* for those who are in the body-state. But the entire sphere of its existence is comprised of energy, and is dominated by energy. All that it can think of or do is in terms of energy and is achieved by means of energy. The energy-state is the state of spiritually *advanced souls*, but it is far from being the state of Perfection, which expresses itself through the *Sahaj Samadhi* of the *Siddha*.

The second important step towards *Sahaj Samadhi* is taken when the soul transcends the domain of energy and enters the domain of mind. *All energy is ultimately an expression of the mind*, there-

Life of the mind

fore the transition from the energy-state to the *mind-state* constitutes a still further advance towards the *God-state* of *Sahaj Samadhi*. In the mind-state, consciousness is directly linked up with the mind, and is in no way fettered by the domination of the body or energy, but is mind-ridden. *Saints* who are in the mind-state can read and influence the minds of others. However, the mind-ridden state is still within the domain of duality and illusion, and it has to be transcended before attainment of union with the Infinite.

The entire advance, from the very beginning, consists in gradually curtailing and transcending the working of the individual mind. The mind is function-

Mind veils the Truth

ing even in the body-state and in the energy-state, but *in the body-state the mind thinks in terms of the body, in the energy-state it thinks in terms of energy, while in the mind-state it thinks in its own terms.* However, even when the mind thinks in its own terms, it does not attain knowledge and realisation of the Infinite, because it becomes its own veil between thought and the Truth. Though the mind may be unencumbered by the life of the body or the life of energy, it is still limited by separative consciousness. It might be compared to a mirror which is covered with dust. The mind has, therefore, to be completely merged and dissolved in the Infinite before it is possible to experience the *God-state* of *Sahaj Samadhi. Form is solidified energy; energy is an expression of mind; mind is the covered mirror of Eternity; and Eternity is Truth which has thrown off the mask of mind.*

To discard the limiting mind is no easy thing. The chief difficulty is that the mind has to be annihilated through the mind itself. Intense longing for

Crossing of mind requires longing and patience

union with the Infinite Reality as well as infinite patience are indispensable in the process of crossing the mind. One Master told his disciple that in order to attain the highest state he had to be thrown, bound hand and foot to a plank, into a river, where he must keep his garments dry. The disciple could not understand the inner meaning of this injunction. He wandered until he encountered another saint and asked him the meaning of the injunction given by the Master. The saint explained that in order to attain God, he had to long intensely for union with Him, as if he could not live another moment without it, and yet to have the inexhaustible patience which could wait for billions of years. If there is lack of intense longing for uniting with God, the mind lapses into its usual *sanskaric* working, and if there is lack of infinite patience, the very longing which the mind entertains sustains the working of the limited mind. *It is only when there is a balance between infinite longing and infinite patience that the aspirant can ever hope to pierce through the veil of the limited mind, and this combination of extremes can only come through the grace of the Master.*

To dwell in *Sahaj Samadhi* is to dwell in Truth-consciousness. This state cannot be grasped by anyone whose mind is working. The *God-state* is beyond the

Self-knowledge of Sahaj Samadhi sustained by effortless intuition

mind, for it dawns when the limited mind disappears in final union with the Infinite. The soul now knows itself *through itself* and not through the mind. The worldly man knows that he is a human being and not a dog. In the same way, in *Sahaj Samadhi*, the soul just knows that it is God and not a finite thing. The worldly man does not have to keep repeating to himself that he is not a dog but a human being; he just knows without having to make any special effort that he is a human being. In the same way the soul, in *Sahaj Samadhi*, does not need any artificial inducing of God-consciousness through repeated auto-suggestions. It just knows itself to be God through *effortless intuition.*

He who has *Sahaj Samadhi* is established in the knowledge of the soul. Knowledge does not come and go, it is permanent. In the state of ignorance the aspirant looks upon himself as a man or woman, as the

Life in eternity

agent of limited actions and the receiver of joys and pains. In the state of knowledge he knows himself as the soul, which is not in any way limited by these things and which is untouched by them. Once he knows his own true nature, he knows it for good and never again becomes involved in ignorance. This state of God-consciousness is infinite, and is characterised by unlimited understanding, purity, love and happiness. *To be initiated in Sahaj Samadhi is to arrive at the endlessness of life in eternity.*

Sahaj Samadhi has two forms: (1) *Nirvana* or absorption in divinity, and (2) *Nirvikalpa* state or divinity in expression. When consciousness is withdrawn

Two forms of *Sahaj Samadhi*

entirely from all the bodies and the world of creation, it leads to *Nirvana* or the *beyond state*, but when consciousness is again made to function through the bodies without attachment or identification, it leads to *Sahaj Samadhi of the Nirvikalpa state or the Sadguru-state. Here, though consciousness is attached to the bodies as instruments, it is detached from them inwardly by non-identification.* The piercing of the mind amounts to the complete withdrawal of consciousness from the universe and its total absorption in God. This is the state where the universe becomes a zero; this is *Nirvana*. Most persons who attain *Nirvana* never come back again to consciousness of the universe. Those few who descend to consciousness of the universe, experience it as nothing but God, and remain constantly in the *Sahaj Samadhi of the Nirvikalpa* state. *Nirvikalpa* state means a life where the mental activity of false imagination has come to an end, and where *the oscillations of the limited mind are all stilled in the realisation of the unchangeable Truth.*

The *Sahaj Samadhi* of the *Nirvikalpa* state comes

to souls who descend from the seventh plane. It belongs to the *Sadgurus* and the *Avatars*. The poise and

State of *Sadgurus* and *Avatars*

harmony of this state remain undisturbed even while giving energetic response to the changing circumstances of life. He who has this state sees God everywhere and in everything, and he sees nothing but God. His God-state is, therefore, in no way toned down while dealing with the things of this world. While drawing the bow or using the sword in the battlefield, while flying in an aeroplane or talking to people, or while engaged in other activities which require the closest attention, he is continuously in the conscious enjoyment of the immutable Truth.

The state of *Nirvana* and the *Nirvikalpa* state are similar to the state of *Mukti* or *Moksha*, representing the merging of the individual soul in God and yielding the

***Moksha, Nirvana* and *Nirvikalpa* state**

eternal bliss and infinite knowledge of super-consciousness. But *Mukti* or *Moksha* is experienced *after* the soul has dropped its body, while the states of *Nirvana* and *Nirvikalpa* can both be experienced *before* giving up the bodies. However, though the states of *Nirvana* and *Nirvikalpa* are similar as to retaining bodies, and though they are also fundamentally the same in essence, there is a slight difference between the two.

When the soul comes out of the ego-shell and enters into the infinite life of God, *its limited individuality is replaced by unlimited individuality*. The soul knows that

Difference between *Nirvana* and the *Nirvikalpa* state

it is God-conscious and thus *preserves its individuality*. The important point is that individuality is not entirely extinguished, but it is retained in the spiritualised form.

However, though the unlimited individuality of the soul is, in a way, retained in the union with the Infinite, *it may remain eternally quiescent in the experience of self-contained divinity*. None comes back to world-consciousness from this state of *Nirvana* or absorption. In a very few cases, however, the soul which has just entered the infinite life of God *establishes its unlimited individuality through the release of dynamic divinity*. This is the *Sahaj Samadhi* of the *Nirvikalpa* state.

The Dynamics of Spiritual Advancement

SPIRITUAL advancement begins when there is a radical change in the outlook of the worldly man. The worldly man lives mostly for the body, and even

Subjugation of body for higher life

in those pursuits which do not seem to have a direct reference to the body, in the last analysis the ultimate motive power is to be found in the desires connected with the body. For example, he lives to eat; he does not eat to live. He has not yet discovered any purpose clearly transcending the body, so the body and its comforts become the centre of all his pursuits. But when he discovers a value in which the soul is predominant, the body is at once relegated to the background. The maintenance of the body now becomes for him merely instrumental for the realisation of a higher purpose. *His body, which had formerly been a hindrance to true spiritual life, becomes an instrument for the release of higher life*. At this stage man attends to his bodily needs with no special feeling of self-identification, but like the driver of a railway engine who fills it with coal and water so that it may be kept going.

The very beginning of spiritual advancement is conditioned by quest for that goal for which man lives—*the goal for which he unconsciously loves and hates, and for*

Quest for the goal *which he goes through variegated joys and sufferings*. Though he may be stirred by the pull of this incomprehensible and irresistible divine destiny, it may take a long time before he arrives at the mountain top of Truth-realisation, and the path is constantly strewn with pitfalls and slippery precipices. Those who attempt to reach this mountain top have to climb higher and higher, and *even if a person has succeeded in scaling great heights, the slightest mistake on his part might cast him down to the very beginning again*. Therefore the aspirant is never safe unless he has the advantage of the help and guidance of a Perfect Master who knows the ins and outs of the path, and who can not only safeguard the aspirant from a possible fall, but lead him to the goal of realisation without unnecessary relapses.

The aspirant who has decided to reach the goal carries with him all the *sanskaras* which he has accumulated in the past, but in the intensity of his spiritual longing they remain suspended and ineffective for the time being. Time and again, however, when there is a slackening of spiritual effort, the *sanskaras* hitherto suspended from action gather fresh strength and, *arraying themselves in a new formation, constitute formidable obstacles in the spiritual advancement of the aspirant*.

Blocking of advancement

This might be illustrated by the analogy of a river. The powerful current of the river carries with it great quantities of silt from the source and the banks. As long as these quantities are suspended in water they do not hinder the flow of the river, though they may slow it down. When the current becomes slower in the plains, and particularly towards the mouth, this bulk tends

Analogy of the river

to deposit in the river bed and to form huge islands or deltas, which not only obstruct the current but often divert it or even split it into smaller currents and, on the whole, weaken the force of the mighty river. Or again, when the river is in flood, it sweeps away all obstacles of trees, bushes and rubbish in its path, but when these accumulate to a certain degree, they can constitute a serious hindrance to the flow of the river. In the same way *the path of spiritual advancement is often blocked by the obstacles of its own creation, and these can be removed only through the help of the Master.*

The help of the Master is most effective when the aspirant surrenders his ego-life in favour of the unlimited life which the Master represents. Complete self-

Egoism must disappear

surrender is most difficult to achieve, and yet the most essential condition of spiritual advancement is the *decreasing of egoism* to its minimum. The objective of spiritual advancement is not so much "works," but quality of life free from ego-consciousness. If the aspirant has many great things to his credit which he has claimed as his, his ego fastens itself upon achievements and this constitutes a formidable hindrance to life unlimited. Hence comes the futility of rituals and ceremonies, acts of charity and good works, external renunciation and penances when rooted in ego-consciousness.

It is, therefore, most necessary for the aspirant to keep free from the idea, "I do this, and I do that." This does not mean that the aspirant is to keep clear of all

The dilemma

activity through fear of developing this form of the ego. He may have to take to the life of action to wear out the ego he has already developed. Thus he is caught up in *the dilemma that if he stays inactive he does nothing to break through the prison of his ego-life, and if he takes to a life of action he is faced with the possibility of his ego being transferred to these new acts.*

For spiritual advancement the aspirant has to *avoid these two extremes* and yet carry on a life of creative action. Treading the spiritual path is not like riding a

Treading the path like walking on edge of a sword

saddled horse, but like walking on the sharp edge of a sword. Once a rider is on horseback he is practically at rest, sitting with more or less ease and requiring very little effort or attention to proceed. Treading the spiritual path, however, requires utmost attention and carefulness since the path affords no halting places or room for expansion of the ego-life. *He who enters the path can neither remain where he is nor can he afford to lose his balance. He is like one who attempts to walk on the sharp edge of a sword.*

To avoid inaction on the one hand and pride of action on the other, it is necessary for the aspirant to construct in the following manner a provisional and

Constructing new ego subservient to Master

working ego which will be entirely subservient to the Master. Before beginning any-

thing, the aspirant thinks that it is not *he* who is doing it, but the *Master* who is getting it done through him. After doing it he does not tarry to claim the results of action or enjoy them, but becomes free of them by offering them to the Master. By training his mind in this spirit he succeeds in creating a new ego which, though provisional and working, is amply able to become a source of that confidence, feeling, enthusiasm and "go" which true action must express. This new ego is spiritually harmless, since it derives its life and being from the Master who represents Infinity, and since, when the time comes, it can be thrown away like a garment. There are thus two types of ego—one which can only add to the limitations of the soul, and the other which helps towards emancipation. The passage through the limiting ego of the worldly man to the egolessness of the infinite life lies through the construction of the provisional ego generated through wholehearted allegiance to the Master. *The construction of a new ego which is entirely subservient to the Master is indispensable to the dynamics of spiritual advancement.*

The aspirant has been accustomed to derive zest in life from his limited ego, and an immediate transition from the life of egoistic action to that of egoless action

Sudden transition to egoless life impossible

is impossible and uninspiring. *If the aspirant were to be immediately required to avoid all forms of ego-consciousness he would have to revert to a state of negative passivity, without any joy of expression. Or, he would have to seek expression through activity which is merely automatic, like that of a lifeless machine, so that he could not derive any sense of fulfillment.* The real problem is that the aspirant has to abandon his life of the limited ego and enter into the limitlessness of the egoless life without lapsing into a *coma*, where there would be an ebbing of all life. Such a coma might give temporary relief from the limitation of the ego-life, but it cannot initiate the aspirant into the infinity of egoless activity.

This is the reason why, in most cases, spiritual advancement has to be very gradual and often takes several lives. Where a person seems to have taken long

Spiritual advancement is gradual

strides in his spiritual advancement he has merely recapitulated the advancement already secured in previous lives, or there has been special intervention by the Master. In normal cases the advancement of the aspirant has to be gradual. *The distance between the limited life of the ego and the limitlessness of the ego-life has to be covered by gradual stages of ego-transformation, so that egoism is replaced by humility, surging desires are replaced by steadily growing contentment, and selfishness is replaced by selfless love.*

When the ego is entirely subservient to the Master it is not only indispensable and spiritually harmless, but is directly contributory to the spiritual advancement of the aspirant because it brings him closer and closer to the Master through the life of selfless service and love.

Ego subservient to Master ensures his help

Constant inward contact with the Master, which it secures, makes him particularly amenable to the special help which the Master alone can give. The aspirant who renounces the life of an uncurbed and separative ego in favour of a life of self-surrender to the Master is, through this new subservient ego, operating as an instrument in the hands of the Master. In reality the *Master* is working through him. Just as an instrument has a tendency to go wrong while being put to use, so the aspirant is also likely to get out of order during his working in the world. From time to time the instrument has to be cleansed, overhauled, repaired and set right. In the same way *the aspirant, who during his work has developed new perversities, entanglements and shelters for the personal ego, has to be put into working order so that he can go ahead.*

The aspirant who enlists in the service of the Master may be compared to the broom with which the Master cleanses the world of its impurities. The broom is bound to accumulate the

Need for recurring contact with Master

dirt of the world, and unless cleansed again and again and given a new tone it becomes less efficient in the course of time. Each time the aspirant goes to the Master it is with fresh spiritual problems. He might have got caught in new entanglements connected with a craving for honour, riches or other worldly things that allure man. If he pursues these he might get them, but he might be far from the goal of experiencing God on Whom he had set his heart. Only through the active intervention of the Master can such spiritual disorders be cured. *This task of curing spiritual diseases is comparable to the performance of an operation by a surgeon* who promptly removes the very cause which may have been sapping the vital energies of a man. If a person develops physical ailments and complaints he must go to the doctor or the surgeon, and if he develops spiritual troubles he must go to the Master. Recurring contact with the Master is most necessary throughout the process of spiritual advancement.

The Master helps the aspirant in his own invincible ways, which have no parallel in the ways of the world. If the aspirant is to be the recipient of this help

Each resurrection of ego needs fresh surrenderance

he must make a real effort to surrender himself to the divine will of the Master. The personal ego which the aspirant renounced in his first surrenderance to the Master may reappear in a new aspect, even within the artificial ego meant to be completely subservient to the Master, and create disorder in its smooth working. Hence this new resurrection of the limited personal ego of the aspirant needs to be counteracted through fresh surrenderance to the Master. The series of successive resurrections of the personal ego have to be accompanied by a series of fresh acts of surrenderance to the

Master.

Progress from one surrender to greater surrender is a progression from a minor conquest to a major one. The more complete forms of surrenderance represent the higher states of conscious-

Last surrenderance is that of separateness

ness since they secure greater harmony between the aspirant and the Master. Thus the infinite life of the Master can flow through the aspirant in more abundant measure. *Spiritual advancement is a succession of one surrender after another until the goal of the final surrenderance of the separate ego-life is completely achieved.* The last surrender is the only complete surrenderance. It is the reverse side of the final union in which the aspirant becomes one with the Master. Therefore, in a sense, *the most complete surrenderance to the Master is equivalent to the attainment of the Truth,* which is the ultimate goal of all spiritual advancement.

The Deeper Aspects of Sadhana

FOR most persons, spiritual *Sadhana* (the path of attainment) consists in the external observance of rituals and ceremonies prescribed by their own religion.

Transition from rituals to deeper aspects of *Sadhana* In the initial stages such observance has its own value as a factor contributing towards self-purification and mental discipline; but ultimately the aspirant has to transcend the phase of external conformity and become initiated into the deeper aspects of spiritual *Sadhana*. When this happens the external aspect of religion falls into the background and the aspirant gets interested in the essentials revealed in all the great religions. *True Sadhana consists in a life which is based upon spiritual understanding,* and it comes to a person who is really keen about spiritual realities.

Sadhana must never be regarded as consisting in the application of rigid laws. In life there cannot be and need not be strict and unrelieved uniformity. In

Diversity of *Sadhanas* the spiritual field there is ample room for *diversity of Sadhanas.* The *Sadhana* which is useful for a particular aspirant is bound to be related to his *sanskaras* and temperament and so, although the spiritual goal for all is the same, the *Sadhana* of a given aspirant may be peculiar to himself. However, since the goal is the same for all, the differences with regard to *Sadhana* are not of vital importance, and *the deeper aspects of Sadhana have importance for all aspirants in spite of their differences.*

Sadhana in the spiritual field is bound to be essentially different from *Sadhana* in the material field, because the end is intrinsically different. The end

Sadhana in spiritual field different from Sadhana in material field

sought in the material field is a product which has its beginning and end in *time*. The end sought in the spiritual field is completeness which transcends

the limitations of time. Therefore in the material field *Sadhana* is directed towards the achievement of something which is yet to be, but *in the spiritual field Sadhana is directed towards the realisation of that which always has been, will ever be and now IS.*

The spiritual goal of life is to be sought in life itself and not outside life, so *Sadhana* in the spiritual field has to be such that it brings one's life closer to the spiritual

Goal of spiritual Sadhana

ideal. *Sadhana* in the spiritual field does not aim at the achievement of a limited ob-

jective which may have its day and then ingloriously disappear forever. It aims at bringing about a radical *change in the quality of life* so that it permanently becomes *an expression of the Truth in the eternal NOW*. *Sadhana* is spiritually fruitful if it succeeds in bringing the life of the individual in tune with the divine purpose, which is to enable everyone to enjoy consciously the *God-state*. *Sadhana* has to be completely adapted to this end.

In the spiritual field every part of *Sadhana* must aim at the realisation of the spiritual goal of *securing godliness in all phases of life;* therefore the different aspects of spiritual *Sadhana* will, from one point of view,

Sadhana merges into its goal

represent different gradations towards spiritual perfection. *Sadhana* is perfect to the extent to which it expresses the spiritual ideal, *i. e.*, the degree to which it resembles the perfect life. Thus the greater the disparity that exists between the *Sadhana* and the ideal at which it aims, the less perfect it is; the less disparity that exists between *Sadhana* and the ideal at which it aims, the more perfect it is. *When Sadhana is perfect or complete it merges into the goal—a spiritually perfect life—so that the division of means and end is swallowed up in an inviolable integrity of indivisible being.*

The relation between spiritual *Sadhana* and the end sought through it may be contrasted with the relation which exists between them in the material field. In the material field the end usually falls more or less entirely outside the *Sadhana* through which it is secured, and there is a clear disparity of nature between *Sadhana* and the end achieved through it. Thus pulling the trigger of a gun may become a means of killing a man, but killing a man is essentially different in kind from the pulling of the trigger. In the spiritual field, however, the *Sadhana* and the end sought through it cannot be completely external to each other, and there is no clear disparity of nature between them. In the spiritual field it is not possible to maintain an unbridgeable gulf between *Sadhana* and the end sought through it. This gives rise to the fundamental *paradox* that, *in the spiritual field, the practising of a Sadhana in itself amounts to a partial participation in the goal.* Thus it becomes intelligible why many of the spiritual *Sadhanas* have to be taken seriously *as if* they were, in themselves, the goal.

Sadhana as partial participation in its goal

In its deeper aspects, spiritual *Sadhana* consists in treading (i) The Path of Knowledge (*Dnyana Marga*), (ii) the Path of Action (*Karma Marga*), and (iii) the

Sadhana through knowledge, action and love

Path of Love or Devotion (*Bhakti Marga*). The *Sadhana* of knowledge finds its expression through (a) the exercise of detachment which is born of true understanding, (b) the different forms of meditation and (c) the constant use of discrimination and intuition. Each of these modes through which spiritual knowledge is sought or expressed requires explanatory comments.

The individual soul is entangled in the world of forms and does not know itself as part and parcel of the being of God. This ignorance constitutes the bondage

Detachment

of the soul, and spiritual *Sadhana* must aim at securing emancipation from this bondage. External renunciation of the things of this world is therefore often counted among the *Sadhanas* which lead to liberation. Though such external renunciation may have its own value, it is not absolutely necessary. What is needed is *internal renunciation of craving* for the things of this world. When craving is given up it matters little whether the soul has or has not externally renounced the things of this world, because the soul has internally disentangled itself from the illusory world of forms and has prepared itself for the state of *Mukti*. *Detachment is an important part of the Sadhana of Knowledge.*

Meditation is another means through which spiritual knowledge is sought. Meditation should not be regarded as some queer pursuit peculiar to dwellers in

Meditation

caves. Every person finds himself meditating on something or another. The difference between such natural meditation and the meditation of the aspirant is that the latter is *systematic and organised thinking about things that have spiritual importance*. Meditation, as *Sadhana*, may be personal or impersonal.

Meditation is personal when it is concerned with some spiritually perfect soul. A suitable object for personal meditation may be taken (according to the inclination of the aspirant) from among the *Avatars* or the Masters of the past or from living Perfect Masters. Through such personal meditation the aspirant imbibes all the divine qualities or the spiritual knowledge of the Master. Since it involves love and self-surrender, *personal meditation invites the grace of the Master which alone can give final realisation*. So the *Sadhana* of personal meditation not only makes the aspirant similar to the Master on whom he meditates, but also prepares his way to *be united with the Master in the Truth*.

Impersonal meditation is concerned with the formless and infinite aspect of God. This may lead a person towards the realisation of the impersonal aspect of God, but on the whole this meditation becomes barren unless the aspirant has been duly prepared by the pursuit of personal meditation and the life of virtue. In the ultimate realisation of infinity there is neither the limitation of personality nor the distinction of the opposites of good and evil. In order to have that realisation one has to pass from the personal to the impersonal and from goodness to God, Who is beyond the opposites of good and evil. Another condition of attaining Truth through impersonal meditation is that the aspirant should be able to make his mind absolutely still. This becomes possible only when all the diverse *sanskaras* (impressions) in the mind have vanished. As the *final wiping out of the sanskaras is possible only through the grace of a Master*, the Master is indispensable for success even along the path of impersonal meditation.

The *Sadhana* of Knowledge remains incomplete unless the aspirant exercises constant discrimination and unveils his highest intuitions. Realisation of God comes to the aspirant who uses discrimination as well as his intuitions about true and lasting values. *Infinite knowledge is latent in everyone but it has to be unveiled. The way to increase knowledge is to put into practice that bit of spiritual wisdom which a person may happen to have.* The teachings which have come to humanity through the Masters of wisdom, and the inborn sense of values which the aspirant brings with himself, shed sufficient light upon the *next* step which the aspirant has to take. The difficult thing is to act upon the knowledge which he has. One of the best methods of adding to one's own spiritual wisdom is to make use of the knowledge which one already has. If *Sadhana* of knowledge is to be fruitful it must be implemented at every step by due emphasis on action. Everyday life must be guided by discrimination and inspired by the highest intuitions.

Use of discrimination and intuition

Karma Yoga or the Path of Action consists in *acting up to the best intuitions of the heart without fear or hesitation.* In *Sadhana* what counts is *practice* and not mere *theory.* Sound practice is far more important than sound theory. Practice which is based upon right knowledge will of course be more fruitful, but *even a mistake in a practical direction may have its own valuable lessons to bring.* Mere theoretical speculation, however, remains spiritually barren, even when it is flawless. Thus a person who is not very learned but who sincerely takes the name of God and does his humble duties wholeheartedly, may actually be much nearer to God than one who knows

Importance of action

all the metaphysics of the world but who does not allow any of his theories to modify his everyday life.

The difference between the comparative importance of theory and practice in the field of *Sadhana* may be brought out by means of a well-known story of an ass. An ass, who was plodding along a path for a long time and was very hungry, happened to see two heaps of grass—one at some distance on the *right* side of the path and the other at some distance on the *left* side of the path. Now the ass thought that it was of utmost importance to be absolutely certain which of the two heaps was clearly the better before he could intelligently decide to go to one heap rather than the other. If he decided without thorough thinking and without having *sufficient* grounds for his preference, that would be impulsive action and not intelligent action. So he first considered the distance at which the two heaps were respectively placed from the path which he was treading. Unfortunately for him, after elaborate consideration, he concluded that the heaps were equally distant from the path. So he wondered if there were some other consideration which might enable him to make a "right" choice and speculated upon the respective sizes of the heaps. Even with this second attempt to be *theoretically sure* before acting his efforts were not crowned with success, because he concluded that both heaps were of equal size. Then, with the tenacity and patience of an ass, he considered other things such as the quality of the grass, but as fate would have it, in *all* the points of comparison which he could think of the two heaps turned out to be equally desirable.

Ultimately it happened that since the ass could not discover any deciding factor which would make his preference appear theoretically sound, he did not go to

Story of an ass

either of the two heaps of grass but went straight ahead, hungry and tired as before and not a whit better off for having come upon two heaps of grass. If the ass had gone to one heap, without insisting upon the theoretical certainty of having chosen wisely, he might perhaps have gone to the heap which was not as good as the other; and despite any mistakes in his intellectual judgment he might have been infinitely better off from a practical point of view. In the spiritual life it is not necessary to have a complete map of the Path in order to begin travelling. On the contrary, insistence upon having such complete knowledge may actually hinder rather than help the onward march. *The deeper secrets of spiritual life are unravelled to those who take risks and who make bold experiments with it.* They are not meant for the idler who seeks guaranties for every step. He who speculates from the shore about the ocean shall know only its surface, but he who would know the depths of the ocean must be willing to plunge into it.

Fulfillment of the *Sadhana* of *Karma Yoga* requires that action should spring from perception of the Truth. Enlightened action does not bind because it is not

Selfless service

rooted in the ego and is selfless. Selfishness represents ignorance, while selflessness is a reflection of the Truth. The real justification for a life of selfless service is to be found in this intrinsic worth of such life and not in any ulterior result or consequence. *The paradox of selfless action is that it actually brings to the aspirant much more than could ever come within the purview of ignorant selfishness.* Selfishness leads to a narrow life which moves round the false idea of a limited and separate individual, but selfless action contributes towards the dissipation of the illusion of separateness and turns out to be the gateway to the unlimited life where there is realisation of *All-*

self-ness. What a person has may be lost and what he desires to have may never come to him, but if he parts with something in the spirit of an offering to God, it has already come back to him. Such is the *Sadhana* of *Karma Yoga*.

Even more important than the *Sadhanas* of Knowledge or Action is *Bhakti* or Love. Love is its own excuse for being. It is complete in itself and does not need to

Love

be supplemented by anything. The greatest saints have been content with their love for God, desiring nothing else. Love is no love if it is based upon any expectation. In the intensity of divine love the lover becomes one with the Divine Beloved. *There is no Sadhana greater than love, there is no law higher than love, and there is no goal which is beyond love, for love in its divine state becomes infinite.* God and love are identical, and one who has divine love already has God.

Love may be regarded as being equally a part of *Sadhana* and a part of the goal; but the intrinsic worth of love is so obvious that it is often considered a mistake

Through effort to effortlessness

to look upon it as a *Sadhana* for some other thing. In no *Sadhana* is the merging in God so easy and complete as in love. When love is the presiding genius the path to Truth is effortless and joyous. As a rule *Sadhana* involves effort and sometimes even desperate effort, as in the case of an aspirant who may strive for detachment in the face of temptations. In love, though, there is no sense of effort because it is spontaneous. Spontaneity is of the essence of true spirituality. The highest state of consciousness, in which the mind is completely merged in the Truth, is known as *Sahajawastha*, the state of unlimited spontaneity in which there is uninterrupted *Self-knowledge. One of the paradoxes connected with spiritual Sadhana is that all effort of the aspirant is intended for arriving at a state of effortlessness.*

There is a beautiful story of a *Kasturi-mriga** which brings out the nature of all spiritual *Sadhana*. Once, while roaming about and frolicking among hills and

Story of Kasturi-mriga

dales, the *Kasturi-mriga* was suddenly aware of an exquisitely beautiful scent, the like of which it had never known. The scent stirred the inner depths of its soul so profoundly that it determined to find its source. So keen was its longing that notwithstanding the severity of cold or the intensity of scorching heat, by day as well as by night, it carried on its desperate search for the source of the sweet scent. It knew no fear or hesitation but undaunted went on its elusive search until, at last, happening to lose its foothold on a cliff, it had a precipitous fall resulting in a fatal injury. While breathing its last the deer found that the scent which had ravished its heart and inspired all these efforts came from its own navel. This last moment of the deer's life was its happiest, and there was on its face inexpressible peace.

All spiritual *Sadhana* of the aspirant is like the efforts of the *Kasturi-mriga*. The final fructification of *Sadhana* involves the *termination of the ego-life* of the as-

Goal of Sadhana is Self-knowledge

pirant. At that moment there is the realisation that he himself has, in a sense, been the object of all his search and endeavour, that all that he suffered and enjoyed—all his risks and adventures, all his sacrifices and desperate strivings—were intended for having true *Self-knowledge* in which *he loses his limited individuality, only to discover that he is really identical with God Who is in everything.*

---

*The deer whose navel yields musk.

LIST OF BOOKS BY THE AUTHOR

GOD SPEAKS
LISTEN HUMANITY
LIFE AT ITS BEST
BEAMS ON THE SPIRITUAL PANORAMA
THE EVERYTHING AND THE NOTHING
DISCOURSES

There are many books about Meher Baba and various phases of his unique work.

For books in foreign languages, especially those of India, please write to Adi K. Irani, King's Rd., Ahmednagar, Maharashtra, India.